GW01452672

From GDPR confusion to
Privacy First Marketing

Vibeke Specht

Automated technology used to analyze text and data in digital form for the purpose of generating information, according to sections 15a, 15b and 15c of the Copyright Act (text and data mining), is prohibited.
© 2025 Vibeke Specht
Portraits: Anne-Grete Pettersen, iamag.dk
Publisher: Lex Futura Scientia, Aarhus, Denmark
Print: Libri Plureos GmbH, Hamburg, Germany
ISBN: 978-87-976438-0-8
First Edition 2025

To Carl
May you and your generation keep
The Matrix sufficiently at bay.

This book contains paintings—portraits—created by my friend, artist and privacy fellow Anne-Grete Pettersen. She captures more in one painting than a thousand images ever could.

iamag.dk

A note on the purpose of this book

This book is written by a practitioner, for practitioners. It aims to translate dense legal frameworks into actionable guidance for marketing professionals who need to understand and comply with privacy regulations in their daily work. While the legal foundations are researched and fact-checked, this is not a legal treatise nor a substitute for professional legal counsel.

The privacy landscape evolves rapidly, with new court decisions, regulatory guidance, and enforcement actions emerging regularly. The information in this book reflects the state of affairs as of, June 2025. For legal questions about compliance obligations of your specific organization, please consult qualified legal counsel familiar with your jurisdiction and circumstances.

My goal is simple: to help fellow marketers see that privacy-first marketing is not just legally necessary—it is good business. The technical complexity shouldn't obscure the fundamental principle at stake: respect for human beings in our digital economy.

Vibeke Specht | CIPP/E

Foreword

I have been looking forward to the publication of *From GDPR Confusion to PRIVACY FIRST Marketing* for quite some time. This book is truly unique: It tackles a complex and often misunderstood field—marketing and data protection—in a way that is clear, engaging, and accessible, without requiring the reader to be a highly specialized lawyer.

I first met Vibeke when, alongside founding my own legal consultancy, Lex Futura, I was working part-time as Director of Digital Compliance at the Danish software company Cookie Information. It did not take long for me to see that Vibeke shared my passion for the intersection of data protection, privacy, and technology. I also quickly discovered that she possesses a rare talent for making sense of a legal area that many find complicated, even intimidating. Vibeke is relentless in her pursuit of clarity; she will not rest until she truly understands a matter, a quality that challenged me, but also broadened my own perspective.

With more than 25 years of professional experience in data protection, spanning academia, private legal practice, in-house roles, and the legal tech industry – I know how difficult it can be not only to understand data protection legislation but also to communicate it effectively. Vibeke has a remarkable gift: She strengthens her own understanding by explaining concepts to others. This gift was evident when she, entirely on her own initiative, created a 40-page booklet to help Cookie Information's customers navigate the key data protection issues relevant to digital marketing.

Data protection in a marketing context can often feel like the Wild West. Traditionally, many marketers have shown little interest in it, seeing legal requirements as constraints on their work. Access to data is central to their daily operations, and consent solutions are sometimes viewed as obstacles that disrupt a website's design. It is easy to deploy analytics tools from global providers while turning a blind eye to whether valid consent has been obtained before the (personal) data is transferred to the global provider. These practices have resulted in non-compliant business models and widespread unlawful processing of personal data. Vibeke decided to take a different path. With the quiet determination of someone who believes things can be done better—and with a touch of Pippi Longstocking's spirit, "I have never tried that before, so I think I would definitely be able to do it"—she set out to write a book showing that different way is possible.

I am deeply impressed by her knowledge and her exceptional ability to communicate the rules from both a practitioner's and a non-lawyer's perspective. This book will be of great value not only to marketing professionals, but also to lawyers who wish to better understand the realities of the marketing world.

During the process of transforming the booklet into a full manuscript, I had discussions with Vibeke. At no point did I doubt that I wanted to publish her work through Lex Futura's newly established publishing arm, Lex Futura Scientia. Fortunately, Vibeke also thought it was a great idea.

Congratulations to Vibeke on her first book—and to all of you who will read it. By the time you turn the final page, you will have moved from GDPR confusion to becoming PRIVACY FIRST marketers.

Charlotte Bagger Tranberg | PhD
CEO at Lex Futura
Aarhus, August 2025

FOREWORD BY CHARLOTTE BAGGER TRANBERG

PART 1: INTRODUCTION
Chapter 1. Unaware
Chapter 2. But who cares?
Chapter 3. The Nazis and personal data

PART 2: THE LAWS
Chapter 4. What is personal data?
Chapter 5. The GDPR explained for marketers
Chapter 6. The lives of others

PART 3: THE COFFEE & THE COOKIES
Chapter 7. What is a cookie?
Chapter 8. The cookie death
Chapter 9. Is the pixel tastier than the cookie?
Chapter 10. Cookie-banner fatigue?

PART 4: DIGITAL ADVERTISING
Chapter 11. Ad fatigue
Chapter 12. The reformed ad-tech addict?
Chapter 13. Browser, browser on the screen
Chapter 14. When tech giants derail capitalism
Chapter 15. The bombers & the blind spot
Chapter 16. To fix what is not broken

PART 5: THE PRIVACY-FIRST BALANCE
Chapter 17. Privacy-first marketing
Chapter 18. The trust factor

I

Introduction

1. Unaware

I'm a Swede. Born and raised in the very south of Sweden where people have this guttural and, shall we say, "relaxed" vernacular. When I was eight, I saw a TV-program about dialects on channel one or two. This was during the 1980s so there were only two Swedish TV-channels to choose between.

The next day one of my classmates, Malin, and I talked about the program. Did we really have an accent? During morning recess we walked over to our teacher Kerstin. She was on playground duty that day. I remember how the southern Swedish drizzle hit us sideways as we looked up at her and in unison, with what must have been the broadest northern Scanian accent ever, asked:

"KeeeRRRstiiin, do we speeeeeak with an acceeeent?"

Kerstin was from the capital region of our country (as I learned many years later), and therefore did not speak with our southern accent.

"YES, of course you DO!", she replied emphatically.

"Ohhhhh," Malin and I said, looking at each other.

I remember how astonished we were. Why had we not "heard" or understood this before?

Two years later, in 1989, computer scientist Tim Berners-Lee developed the HTTP protocol, which, together with the HTML language, laid the foundation for the World Wide Web and thus, opened the door to perhaps the greatest information technology revolution of our time.

Neither my friend Malin nor I had any idea about this, of course.

The web, which we sometimes misleadingly call the internet, was initially a system where users navigated from one static webpage to another using a browser. This early "Web 1.0" gradually evolved into a blog- and social media-centered Web 2.0, characterized by interactive platforms and digital advertising ecosystems. Today, we are still largely operating within this environment, even as discussions about the need for a new kind of web has been going on: a decentralized Web 3.0, designed to reduce the dominance of large tech companies and to create a more open, well-functioning digital marketplace.

The store that knew when their customers were pregnant

As far as I can remember, I did not come into any meaningful contact with the web until high school when we could go to the computer lab and chat on ICQ.

The dot-com crash was certainly hard to miss, but the first time I truly took notice of an internet-based news story was in 2012, when The New York Times revealed how the American retail chain Target was profiling its customers and their purchasing habits.

By analyzing shopping patterns, Target could determine if a teenage girl was pregnant before she had fully realized it herself, and definitely before she had informed anyone else in her household. Target acted on this information by sending tailored advertisements (in form of coupons by snail mail) for products that an expectant parent might need. When the girl's father confronted Target, demanding to know why they had taken the liberty to send baby-related advertising to his daughter, the situation became, well, awkward.

The story of the teenage girl and her unsuspecting father became global news. It sparked a debate about how the digital environments we navigate as consumers can seize and use information about us without our awareness or understanding of how or why.

The Target story was neither the first nor the last eye-opener in the ongoing narrative about the risks that the web carries. Long before 2012, around the turn of the millennium, another story made headlines. The world's then-largest ad-tech company —DoubleClick—was accused of combining tracking data they had collected via cookies with other personally identifiable information they had acquired by purchasing the ad-tech company Abacus Direct—to identify and profile people at a remarkably detailed level. DoubleClick's plans outraged consumer rights groups and the general public. Many believed that DoubleClick's actions constituted a serious invasion of privacy, as users had not been informed about or consented to such extensive tracking, data sharing, and profiling.

Six years later, in 2006, the American web company AOL accidentally published the search history of hundreds of thousands of its users. Even though the data was considered anonymized, users could still be identified.[1] The case highlighted how much can be revealed about an individual simply by studying what he or she searches for on the web.

The following year, around Christmas 2007, Facebook introduced a feature they called Beacon.[2] It allowed websites to tell your friends and family (on Facebook) if, for example, you had bought a pair of red shoes or a video game.

Why did websites choose to send this kind of information to Facebook? Because they got the opportunity then to advertise their services "for free" on the platform.

Facebook was accused of violating people's privacy and spoiling Christmas gift surprises. It was possible to turn off the Beacon feature, but the system required users to actively choose to turn off the function if they did not want it – instead of actively opting-in to turn it on. Facebook also made little effort to easily inform and guide users to the control panel for this feature. For those familiar with the first major Facebook pixel[3]

---

[1] A former CIA worker says he leaked surveillance data, *The New York Times*, 9 August 2006, https://www.nytimes.com/2006/08/09/technology/09aol.html
[2] The Evolution of Facebook's Beacon, *The New York Times*, 29 November 2007, https://archive.nytimes.com/bits.blogs.nytimes.com/2007/11/29/the-evolution-of-facebooks-beacon/
[3] IMY decisions regarding the use of Meta Pixel: Kry International AB (reprimand), Apohem AB (fine: 12 million SEK), Apoteket AB (fine: 37 million SEK, appealed), Apotea AB (fine: 7.5 million SEK), Avanza Bank AB (fine: 15 million SEK, appealed), Länsförsäkringar AB (fine: 35 million

cases handled by the Swedish data protection authority, this negligence of Facebook seems familiar.

The feature caused significant controversy. The pressure from public opinion and the American class action lawsuit led Facebook to retire the feature and establish a fund of several million dollars for online privacy and security.

Target, DoubleClick, and Beacon are just a few examples of historical events that drew attention to the fact that the web was a place where companies were willing to track people, with minimal transparency, in ways few of them would have been comfortable doing in a physical store. It appears they were presumably guided by the notion "if it is possible, it is permissible."

Ground zero for the privacy issue

In June 2013, a bombshell dropped that would forever change our understanding of the internet, Web 2.0, and the value of personal data.

From a hotel room in Hong Kong, Edward Snowden, a then systems administrator at the National Security Agency (NSA) revealed that the American government, through NSA, was conducting mass surveillance on an unprecedented scale. With the courage of his convictions and thousands of classified documents in hand, Snowden approached journalists to expose what he believed the world needed to know.[4]

It was not just the scale of government surveillance that was shocking, but also how deeply it had penetrated the digital services people use every day. Nine of America's tech giants—including Google, Facebook, Microsoft, Amazon, and Apple—were implicated. Through a program called PRISM, formally

---

SEK); Swedish Authority for Privacy Protection (IMY), 2024. Search for each case at https://www.imy.se/tillsyner
[4] *The New York Times*, 10 June 2013, https://www.nytimes.com/2013/06/10/us/former-cia-worker-says-he-leaked-surveillance-data.html

operating under Section 702 of the Foreign Intelligence Surveillance Act, the NSA was collecting emails, video chats, voice calls, photographs, and documents. All without the public's knowledge and consent.[5]

When confronted, the tech companies issued carefully worded denials, claiming they only provided data when legally compelled. But the damage was done. The veil had been lifted, revealing an uncomfortable truth: Our private digital lives were anything but private. The outrage was global, crossing borders and political divides, as citizens and governments alike grappled with the implications.

People began questioning the tech giants themselves: If the NSA could access all these data, just how much information were these companies collecting—and what were they doing with it? For the first time, the public glimpsed the vast ocean of personal data being harvested from their online activities—data available not just to governments, but to countless corporate interests.

As pressure mounted on tech companies to answer for their data practices, momentum began building for regulatory reform. This groundswell culminated three years later, in 2016, in the European Parliament passing the General Data Protection Regulation (GDPR) with overwhelming support—the most comprehensive privacy legislation the world had ever seen.

Several years have passed since Malin and I stood in the schoolyard pondering accents. I have grown up and found myself working in what they call the creative industries, slowly and reluctantly coming to a strange realization: The child who once could not hear her own Scanian accent, had become the marketer who did not realize she was fluent in "cookie-ish."

This, to be honest, is far more incredible than missing your own dialect. After all, I had been following the debates on digital privacy. I, too, was horrified by Target, Facebook

---

[5] PRISM, *Wikipedia*, https://en.wikipedia.org/wiki/PRISM

Beacon, and PRISM. And yet, there I was, writing ad copy for Facebook, ordering retargeting campaigns, and setting up HubSpot flows. It is a kind of willful blindness that, in hindsight, feels as absurd as waking up one day and suddenly noticing that my house has plumbing.

I suppose I was living with cognitive dissonance. Hence, when the GDPR landed—despite it happening in the wake of the aforementioned scandals—my marketing team and I had little desire to understand what it was about. For us, it was just "more work."

Do you remember, for instance, the run-up to the GDPR in spring 2018? Name a marketer who was not sitting there, structuring email flows and sending countless reminder emails to every lead in the CRM system.

We had a lawyer who updated our privacy policy and explained the importance of obtaining consent from all contacts in the CRM system, and that was what we acted on. We were told to collect consent from every contact in our system: Those who did not agree to stay, or did not respond, had not given their consent and should be deleted. Period. The question did not extend further than that in our company or in our marketing department. No one talked about the cookie issue, for example, which also needed review, least of all me.

I simply did not realize I was speaking fluent cookie-ish and fueling our tools with personal data every day. And it would take a while before that penny dropped.

A slow awakening

After ten years in the marketing field, I decided to get a Google Analytics certification. Around the same time, I landed a new job in Denmark where I was taken aback.

At this job, I had a brilliant colleague called Mona. Mona was highly knowledgeable about the GDPR and responsible for setting up the company's CRM system. Something that, as Mona emphasized, could not be done in a long-term sustainable way without making the system GDPR-compliant, so that personal data (such as email addresses, phone numbers, and more) were collected, stored, and deleted in a systematic manner.

She was right, of course.

But before I met Mona, I had not given digital privacy very deep thought, that is, unless you count the "obsessive thoughts" during the spring of 2018. Please note that the company I joined had not at all worked with digital marketing before. This was a golden opportunity to set everything up the right way from the get-go: From which web platform we should have, to which digital services we should use. The field was wide open. Mona therefore asked me which analytics tool we should use.

"What do you mean?"

"Well, we do not have to use Google Analytics."

"What do you mean, "not Google Analytics?", I asked.

I was stunned. I had just gotten my GA license, and now this person was suggesting we might not use GA, like, at all.

"What would we use then?", I wondered aloud.

It fell on my desk to investigate what the alternatives were.

Now, it was not that Mona flatly refused Google Analytics. It was possible, she said, to configure the settings so we could use GA without sending identifiable personal data to the company's American servers.

It was like slowly turning my head toward one of my blind spots and thinking, "oh." Edward Snowden's revelation was no longer "just" an upsetting geopolitical issue at a comfortable distance from my immediate everyday life.

Despite this growing awareness, my first encounter with the privacy issue and its impact on digital marketing remained fairly superficial. I was not all-in, so to speak. I had become somewhat more conscious and had begun to develop an emotional understanding of why these questions were indeed important. At the same time, my job was to bring in leads, to craft content that would engage readers and drive conversions.

It was not in my immediate interest to limit my options by insisting on a cookie banner or protesting the Facebook pixel, for example, that is, until eventually, it was in my immediate interest.

The turning point came when I began working for a Danish company in the privacy-tech sector—a software company offering cookie compliance solutions. They needed help making privacy technology and the legal frameworks underlying their solution more understandable for the Swedish market. I thought it sounded interesting, so I rolled up my sleeves and dove down the rabbit hole.

Somewhere during my journey at the company, winding through underground passages of articles, legal paragraphs, and interviews with subject matter experts, I paused and decided to document this mapping process. This was in 2022, and I solemnly swore I would finish the book before the end of the year. Initially, I just wanted to create a practical guide. But the more I learned, the more experts I spoke with, the more impossible it became to limit the project to a handy little marketer's pocket guide.

The question of how to successfully conduct Privacy First Marketing turned out to be not only more complex than I had hoped, but also intimately connected with the survival of free journalism and the integrity of our shared information ecosystem.

The crux of the matter was not the GDPR or other data protection legislations. The real issue was the entities, the monopolies that pretended they were not, even though they control the web as an advertising and marketing space, establishing unwritten rules that all marketers around the world are forced to navigate daily.

I found myself in yet another "do-we-speak-with-an-accent" moment. This is why this book is not just a (hopefully) accessible account of how marketers can become more privacy-friendly, but also a story about how we are now witnessing the potential end of a 25-year-old era where tech giants like

Alphabet and Meta have grown to dominate the web—and how their days of unchallenged power seem numbered.

2. But who cares?

Quite a few from the looks of it.

Seven years have passed since GDPR took effect, and the indifference among Swedish and international marketers is no longer quite so laissez-faire. Max Schrems, GDPR's unofficial poster boy and founder of the privacy rights organization Noyb (None of Your Business), is no longer completely unknown outside privacy circles in my country. Especially not since they sued Sweden for allowing services like Mr. Koll.[6]

As of this writing (fall 2024), Noyb is also pursuing a case against the Swedish Data Protection Authority (IMY). Noyb accuses IMY of routinely avoiding its investigative obligations.[7]

Besides this, it feels at times like million-euro fines have been raining down on companies that violate the General Data Protection Regulation—even for missteps in seemingly trivial matters like cookie compliance.

In Sweden, as mentioned, five Facebook pixel cases have led to substantial penalty fees for website owners who used Meta's service. That it has become harder to keep pretending everything is fine, was also made clear in the summer of 2023 when IMY announced that four audited companies had to stop using Google Analytics in its existing configuration due to GDPR compliance issues and would only be allowed to resume its use if they could ensure proper safeguards and adjustments.[8]

And to top it all off, there is the saga about the third-party cookie-phase-out in Google's Chrome browser, which seemed like an never-ending story until it was not, and Apple's aggressive tracking restrictions in Safari. It is not a stretch to

---

[6] Noyb, (source retrieved November 2024), https://noyb.eu/en/swedish-data-brokers-claim-journalists-legal-protection-evade-eu-law

[7] Noyb, (source retrieved November 2024) https://noyb.eu/en/noyb-takes-swedish-dpa-court-refusing-properly-deal-complaints

[8] IMY, (source retrieved November 2024) https://www.imy.se/nyheter/fyra-bolag-maste-sluta-anvanda-google-analytics

say that the web as we marketers know it was undergoing a tectonic shift even before the AI-LLM-bonanza started to go into overdrive.

Meanwhile, consumers were becoming increasingly aware. There has been no shortage of reports from major consulting firms and institutions measuring consumer trust—or the lack thereof—in how websites and platforms handle their personal data. As one Swedish citizen put it in a 2022 Google study on privacy and marketing:

I know my data is very valuable, and I want to control whose hands it ends up in.[9]

Awareness has risen across the board. This is driving companies, website owners, and indeed marketers, to take a hard look at their digital house and examine what kinds of services, pixels, and scripts they have chosen to run on their properties. This is undoubtedly a positive development because it lays the foundation for a more trustworthy web. Even if we do not think about it every day, trust is the bedrock of the web as a marketplace. It always has been for any marketplace, really.[10] Without trust, the web becomes dysfunctional. And nobody benefits from that.

Does this mean the party is over?

It means that partying on free personal data does not have a future. Or, to put it bluntly: Stealing personal data and profiling people without their consent, or storing personal information without legal grounds, is no longer something only regulators care about.

---

[9] Google/Ipsos, *Privacy by design: the benefits of putting people in control – Sweden edition*, July 2022, p. 10, Ipsos and Google, July 2022, available as PDF.

[10] See for example Greif, A. (2000). *The Fundamental Problem of Exchange: A Cognitive Approach*. Stanford University.
https://web.stanford.edu/~avner/Greif_Papers/2000%20EREH%20Fundament al%20Problem.pdf

As companies and marketers, you now have to earn and protect the personal data your followers and potential customers choose to share with you. The trust you build here is absolutely critical to your long-term credibility. I would go so far as to argue that this is a social sustainability issue—one you can legitimately integrate into your sustainability reporting or highlight when discussing how you are working toward the UN's Sustainable Development Goals.

At the same time, however, the power and responsibility do not rest entirely with you as an individual marketer, brand, or company. You noticed that the quote above came from a Google report, right? It certainly seems ironic that Google, in this context, appears to have been taking—and continues trying to take —the high road on data protection issues. Not just through hefty Think with Google reports,[11] but also by packaging products like Google Consent Mode and the Chrome third-party cookie phase-out as principled compliance measures. This also speaks to how unavoidable and crucial privacy and integrity have become today. It reveals just how inescapable the topic is when a giant—whose business model is built on hoarding as much personal data as possible—feels compelled to take a stance and offer "solutions" to the dilemma of privacy-friendly advertising and marketing.

However, it is obviously just a smokescreen. Trying to have your cake and eat it too, is not an easy equation, not even for one of the world's most powerful companies.

One of the hardest things during my journey as a privacy advisor and marketer in the privacy-tech space has been coming to terms with how everyone in the marketing industry (even at a dedicated privacy-tech company) *and* the publishing world are so incredibly dependent on staying in Google's good graces. When they release reports on the topic, for instance, we

---

[11] Think with Google, (2021), *Research: Customer privacy practices for building trust*. https://www.thinkwithgoogle.com/intl/en-emea/future-of-marketing/privacy-and-trust/research-customer-privacy-practices/

instinctively react by using them as leverage to sell more consent banners or cookie banners.

But does that mean Google is part of the solution to the surveillance problem and the lack of respect for people's right to privacy online?

This question makes me realize that the forest I could not see for all the trees throughout my working life has largely been called Google,[12] and that my own blind spot—as well as that of others—has served the "forest's" interests. Maybe it is not coincidental at all that the discourse never really gained momentum—GDPR notwithstanding—at least until now? As I write this, a historic antitrust lawsuit against Google LLC is underway in the US where the company is accused of abusing its dominant position in the digital advertising market.

This "trial of the century" in the tech world has revealed with painful clarity how Google has systematically worked to cement its absolute position in advertising and media buying. The numbers speak for themselves: 91 percent of all publishers use Google Ads to display advertisements, and 87 percent depend on Google Ads to reach their audience.

By controlling both the demand and supply sides as well as the largest ad exchange in the market, Google has been able to drive down ad prices for publishers while simultaneously raising prices for advertisers and taking an even bigger cut for sitting in the middle. The result has been a dramatic decline in ad revenue for news organizations and other publishers, contributing to layoffs, closures, and a general impoverishment of investigative journalism, particularly at the local level.

As I said, the heart of the matter in pursuing privacy-friendly marketing was not GDPR or other data protection laws. The heart of the matter was the company that refused to call itself a monopoly.

Yet even as monopolistic practices of the tech giants remain the central challenge, the European Union continues to

---

[12] And Meta, Amazon, and the other tech-oligopolies.

demonstrate its commitment to protecting individual rights through new legislation. The AI Act, which began its phased implementation in 2024, represents the next step in this rights-based approach. Just as GDPR established that individuals have fundamental rights over their personal data, the AI Act enshrines the principle that people have a right to understand and challenge algorithmic decisions that affect their lives.

What strikes me about the focus of the AI Act on transparency requirements and individual protection is that it shows EU lawmakers are not just reacting to past surveillance harms—they are getting ahead of emerging threats like algorithmic manipulation and automated decision-making. Thus, it is merely another example of legislation that puts human dignity and individual agency at the center, even as technology grows more complex and potentially more invasive.

But do not get me wrong here. GDPR still plays the starring role in this story. In my opinion, it is one of the most beautiful pieces of legislation on earth, because it is so deeply rooted in legal principles that protect every individual's right to privacy. And that makes it, in many ways, a straightforward law to embrace. The more you understand how this law is constructed, the less strange it seems that it is precisely websites, cookies, and the adtech industry that have been in the crosshairs of regulators across Europe.

The power to persuade people by surveilling, tracking, and profiling individuals without their knowledge is not just a harmless business practice for someone trying to sell a pair of red shoes; it is a tool of influence that has also been used by actors who want to affect which party these individuals vote for, get them to gamble more if they are inclined to do so, or keep them scrolling deeper into a (mis)information feed. Our responsibility as marketers is to understand where we fit into this ecosystem and how we can act not only to stay on the right side of the law, but also to make ethical decisions that align with what we want our brands to stand for. All while remaining successful marketers, of course.

With that said, let us ease into the story of ground zero for data protection legislation by taking a trip back in time.

3. The Nazis & personal data

Now we're in that sweet period where everyone agrees that our recent horrors should never be repeated. But collective thinking is usually short-lived. We're fickle, stupid beings with poor memories and a great gift for self-destruction. Although who knows? Maybe this will be it, Katniss.

Plutarch Heavensbee, in *The Hunger Games* by Suzanne Collins

How do you find a human being?

That the German National Socialist regime during the 1930s and 40s systematically tracked and registered people to identify those considered "less valuable" or "undesirable" is a well-documented historical fact. But how exactly did officials of the regime go about this task?

The most obvious answer is population registration systems. The more comprehensive and detailed such registries were, the easier it became for the regime to identify who was who, where they lived, and so on. Historian Bob Moore, for example, describes how the Nazis drew enormous benefit from well-developed and comprehensive population registration system in the Netherlands to persecute its Jewish population. As an occupying power, they found the local authorities and their registries remarkably efficient for locating the people they wanted to target, which resulted in a higher proportion of Jews being deported from the Netherlands compared to other occupied countries in Western Europe.[13]

For the purposes of the Nazi regime, the level of detail in these population registration systems was crucial. Typical information in these registers included not only names and addresses, but often birth dates, occupations, family relationships, and—critically—religious affiliation. Germany had required the registration of religious affiliation since 1875,

---

[13] Moore, Bob, *Survivors: Jewish Self-Help and Rescue in Nazi-Occupied Western Europe* (2010)

giving the regime a ready-made starting point for identifying Jewish citizens. Centralization and standardization of these registries played an equally crucial role. Since the population registration system in Germany was already a well-organized, nationwide network before the Nazis came to power, the information was uniform and easily accessible, enabling large-scale analysis and categorization of the population.

It is also important to highlight how technology amplified the Nazis' capabilities. Edwin Black explains how punch card machines revolutionized the handling of personal data. These machines—early predecessors to computers—were introduced in Germany in the early 1930s and could rapidly sort and analyze millions of personal records.[14]

When the regime introduced new laws in 1935, two years after coming to power, requiring precise racial classification of the population—the so-called Nuremberg Laws—an even greater need for detailed data collection and analysis emerged. Punch card machines became essential for processing the enormous amount of information required for this classification. The laws defined who would be persecuted, while technology gave the regime the tools to efficiently identify and track these individuals. This interplay between law and technology illustrates how quickly seemingly neutral administrative tools can be transformed into instruments of systematic persecution.

It is crucial to note that the Nazi regime's tracking and surveillance system for "finding a human being" was the result of a gradual process that became increasingly sophisticated and brutal over time.[15]

Beyond existing technology and administrative systems, they developed new methods for their purposes. To implement

---

[14] Black, Edwin, *IBM and the Holocaust* (2001)

[15] Historians Götz Aly and Karl Heinz Roth trace in *The Nazi Census: Identification and Control in the Third Reich* (2004) how the regime developed systematic techniques to track and control populations, evolving from basic census methods to advanced technological systems for registration and identification.

the Nuremberg Laws, for example, so-called "Aryan certificates" were introduced, forcing all German citizens to prove their "Aryan" ancestry.

This led to the creation of extensive family trees and genealogical records used to trace Jewish ancestry. Those identified as Jews, who therefore could not obtain an "Aryan certificate," were from September 1941 forced to wear a yellow Star of David visibly sewn onto their outer clothing and carry special identity cards marked with a "J." Beyond this, the regime employed informants and, for the time, sophisticated surveillance methods, including telephone wiretapping and mail monitoring through the secret police, the Gestapo.

After the fall of Nazi Germany in 1945, the country was divided into four occupation zones controlled by the Allied powers: the United States, Britain, France, and the Soviet Union. In 1949, this division led to Germany being split into two states: West Germany and East Germany.

State surveillance continued in East Germany, now under communist rule. The East German security service, the Stasi, built upon many of the surveillance methods that the Gestapo had in its toolkit.[16] For example, the Stasi employed a network of informants that permeated all levels of society.

In West Germany, however, the experiences of the Nazi era and awareness of ongoing surveillance in East Germany led to increased consciousness about the need to protect every individual's privacy.

The country developed comprehensive data protection laws during the 1970s—first in the form of the world's first modern data protection law at the state level in Hesse in 1970, followed by federal legislation in 1977. Six years later, in 1983, the West German Constitutional Court made a groundbreaking decision. In the so-called "census case," the court established the right to "informational self-determination" as a fundamental right derived from the constitution of West Germany. This meant the

---

[16] See also Chapter 8, which covers GDPR's cousin, the ePrivacy Directive, and its connection to surveillance in East Germany.

country affirmed that individuals had the right to control their personal data, that is, whether it could be disclosed and what it could be used for.

The census case arose when the West German government in the early 1980s planned a comprehensive census that would collect detailed information about the population, including personal data, employment information, housing conditions, and more. This initiative led to major protests and legal challenges, as the demands felt "East German-like" and understandably echoed life during the Second World War and its lead-up. When the court examined whether the census initiative was compatible with the constitution, it concluded that it was partially incompatible with two constitutional articles concerning protection of human dignity and the right to free development of personality.[17]

The court determined that if individuals did not have the right to control their personal data, they might refrain from exercising other fundamental rights out of fear of surveillance. The scope of this decision cannot be overstated—it meant that data protection was recognized as a fundamental right in West Germany. Overall, the country adopted a proactive stance on data protection; it was no longer about passing laws that prohibited abuse, but about preventing personal data from falling into the wrong hands in the first place. This approach to privacy and data handling quickly spread beyond the borders of West Germany and influenced the attitude toward data protection in other European countries.[18] And from the early

---

[17] For a detailed analysis of the census case and its significance for data protection in Germany, see Hornung, G. and Schnabel, C. (2009) 'Data protection in Germany I: The population census decision and the right to informational self-determination', *Computer Law & Security Review*, 25(1), pp. 84–88.

[18] But the idea of privacy as a fundamental right did not begin with the German case. Privacy had already been recognized as a basic human right in international agreements like the Universal Declaration of Human Rights (1948) and the European Convention on Human Rights (1950). Later, the OECD established privacy principles in 1980, and in 1981, the Council of

1990s, European institutions began developing harmonized data protection standards, which culminated when the EU adopted the Data Protection Directive in 1995 (Directive 95/46/EC), a significant step toward creating common rules within the EU.[19]

Part of what made the 1995 directive so cutting-edge was how it introduced groundbreaking concepts such as requirements for unambiguous consent for data collection (and explicit consent for sensitive data), the right to be informed about how one's personal data is used, the right to access and correct personal information, and limitations on how long data could be stored. (Concepts that also became inherent parts of the GDPR when it replaced the Data Protection Directive in 2018.) And by doing so these embody or capture the essence of that crucial German legal principle of "informational self-determination" set out in that West German Constitutional court back in 1983.[20]

Europe adopted Convention 108—the first binding treaty just for data protection. That is also why January 28 is celebrated as Data Protection Day in the EU.

[19] Although the European Union (EU) was established by the Maastricht Treaty in 1993, the legal acts adopted before and after that date—including Directive 95/46/EC—were issued under the name European Community (EC), which was the first pillar of the EU responsible for economic and social legislation. It was only after the Treaty of Lisbon in 2009 that the EU became a single legal entity, and legislation since then, such as the GDPR, is cited with the EU designation instead of EC.

[20] Informational self-determination is a translation of the German concept informationelle Selbstbestimmung. It was defined by the German Federal Constitutional Court as the individual's right to essentially determine for themselves the disclosure and use of their personal data. See Hornung, G. and Schnabel, C. (2009) 'Data protection in Germany I: The population census decision and the right to informational self-determination', *Computer Law & Security Review*, 25(1), pp. 84–88. Also see German Federal Constitutional Court, December 15, 1983, 1 BvR 209/83 et al., BVerfGE 65, 1, English translation available at: https://freiheitsfoo.de/census-act/

"Above Europe"

During my second year of high school, our class received an exchange student from the United States. Her name was Denise. Denise told us she had dreamed of coming to Europe, but not "above Europe," as she put it—which made the class chuckle. Sweden had not been her first choice, in other words, but she was pleasantly surprised, nonetheless. The medieval town of Söderköping, where our high school was located, had residential buildings that were older than her entire nation, which she found deeply fascinating.

Denise never elaborated on her "above Europe" comment to the class, and probably none of us thought much more about it at the time. But I cannot help feeling, all these years later, that her little aside perfectly captures Sweden's relationship with Europe in general and the European Union in particular. And think this is a distinctly Swedish characteristic, not a Nordic one.

I do not think it was coincidence that my first real GDPR awakening happened in Denmark. Or as I once pointed out in frustration to a Danish colleague, who could not understand why dealing with Swedish regulatory authorities was more difficult: "Denmark is not Sweden." Allow me to generalize:

o   Denmark has Lego. Sweden has IKEA.
o   Denmark has Mærsk. Sweden had Volvo.
o   Denmark has major privacy-tech companies. Sweden was the first in the Nordics with Facebook's server farms in Norrland.
o   And my favorite: Sweden had Ylva Johansson as EU Commissioner. Denmark had Margarethe Vestager.

Johansson and Vestager can be seen as unwitting archetypes of their respective countries. While Johansson has tried to push through legislation that would essentially enable mass surveillance of EU citizens through the now-infamous "Chat

Control" proposal, Vestager's work to rein in tech giants and protect users' rights has given her near-cult status far beyond data protection circles. It is like night and day—and perfectly aligned with my own experience of how these two neighboring countries differ.

After living in Denmark for several years and working on GDPR issues alongside colleagues responsible for the Danish, Norwegian, and Finnish markets, I have found the distinct approaches of the Nordic countries to their relationship with the EU and data protection fascinating. While my Norwegian colleague quickly became best friends with officials at the Data Protection Authority in Norway—both because she's incredibly intelligent and socially skilled—I felt like Harry Potter approaching Gringotts when dealing with the Swedish Privacy Protection Authority (IMY) and the Swedish Post and Telecom Authority (PTS). And while the Danish Data Protection Authority stepped in and published a comprehensive cookie guideline for website owners in 2020 (even though the subject matter was not on their table) the Swedish IMY has been reluctant to state "what applies" without having a concrete, hyper-specific decided case to reference. This is not because the people I have had the honor of getting to know and working with are not both pleasant and extremely competent. My point is that the more I have worked on these issues with the respective authorities, the more I have experienced Denmark (and Norway) as having a more principled, open, and integrated approach to EU (or EEA) cooperation in general and data protection issues in particular. That Noyb, as mentioned, is now suing the Swedish Data Protection Authority for failing to fulfill its investigative duties is, in my opinion, not surprising. What is strange is that these observations do not align with how Denmark often appears or has been portrayed in Swedish political discourse (at least historically), where the country is often described as more protectionist and EU-critical than Sweden.

As a Swede living in Denmark, I believe this debate says more about Sweden's self-image than about Denmark. It is perhaps an unspoken identity rooted in the historical DNA of being a "moral superpower" or "the world's conscience." This self-image has, like the value of the Swedish krona, weakened considerably over the past decade. Nevertheless, I believe the blind spots and institutional deadlocks that characterize Swedish data protection administration can partly be traced to this historical variable. The result is a country that unconsciously maintains a kind of "neutral" distance and remains above Europe.[21]

Sweden was "neutral" during the war

There is an old TV clip from the mid-1990s on YouTube[22], where journalist Stina Dabrowski interviews former British Prime Minister Margaret Thatcher. In the clip, Dabrowski tries to pressure Thatcher into saying that she thinks the British people are superior, or "better as a people":

Stina: But what I hate more than anything else is what Hitler stood for.
Thatcher: Did you fight against him?
Stina: I was not born then…
Thatcher: Did your people fight against him?
Stina: I wish we had ...

---

[21] For an analysis of Sweden's foreign policy role and self-image during the Cold War, see for example Bjereld, U., Johansson, A.W., & Molin, K., *Sveriges säkerhet och världens fred: svensk utrikespolitik under kalla kriget* (Sweden's Security and World Peace: Swedish Foreign Policy During the Cold War), (2008). The authors discuss Sweden's evolution from a cautious stance to a more active role as a moral superpower, particularly during the 1960s and 70s.

[22] Dabrowski, Stina. Margaret Thatcher – The 'Iron Lady' on power, feminism and the Falklands War, YouTube. Published December 12, 2013. https://youtu.be/p_gnhy7eT1s?feature=shared

Thatcher: So, you admit that it was actually the United States, Canada, and Britain who stormed the beaches of Normandy, while France was defeated, and Italy and Spain laid under fascist dictatorships. You admit all this but object to us claiming we were better? I mean we were better at standing up to tyranny.

[...]

Thatcher: It was the Anglo-American alliance that stood up to tyranny. So did Norway, and Denmark too.

Stina: What do you think of Sweden?

Thatcher: Sweden was neutral.

Stina: What do you think of Sweden?

Thatcher: I think that if people had been neutral towards Hitler, then Hitler would have won.

Dabrowski's questions reflect the Swedish self-image of that era, but Thatcher doesn't buy into the premises of the questions—which not only makes Stina Dabrowski sweat but also cracks the veneer of Sweden as a non-aligned global conscience. In a single brief exchange, the Swedish self-image of internationalism and moral leadership stands in stark contrast to how we acted when it really mattered. When our neighbors Denmark and Norway were occupied, Sweden chose to remain neutral.

Sweden's neutrality during World War II mercifully protected us from direct experiences of surveillance and oppression, but it also contributed to a complex post-war understanding. Some scholars argue that Sweden's subsequent role as a moral conscience was partly a way of dealing with the implicit guilt that arose from our neutrality policy and the subsequent "non-alignment"[23] during the Cold War—a policy

---

[23] For an in-depth analysis of Sweden's neutrality policy during World War II and its aftermath, see Lödén, Hans, *För säkerhets skull: ideologi och säkerhet i svensk aktiv utrikespolitik 1950–1975* (For Security's Sake: Ideology and Security in Swedish Active Foreign Policy 1950–1975), (2005). Originally

that during the war allowed Sweden to continue exporting strategic resources like iron ore and ball bearings to Nazi Germany, without fully confronting the ethical implications of the trade.

According to some analysts, these historical contexts have, ultimately contributed to shaping a peculiar insider-outsider mentality[24] in the relationship of the Swedish nation-state with the European Union. This is an ambivalence that can still be manifested today in tone-deaf legislative proposals, like EU Commissioner Ylva Johansson's Chat Control, or in an institutionally vague approach to data protection issues. This is unfortunate because so many aspects of our (digitized) lives are permeated by technical surveillance, profiling, and tracking on a scale that neither the Stasi, Gestapo, nor the Nazi regime could have dreamed of. The importance of all member states adopting a principled stance in accordance with the regulation in question has never been more urgent—not least from a cybersecurity perspective.

On the other hand, Sweden does have a strong history with data protection legislation, which begs me to nuance the picture. After all, Sweden was the first country in the world to adopt a national data protection law (the Data Act, which took effect on July 2, 1974). And for a time, the Data Inspection Board (today's IMY) was a leading authority in Scandinavia. Many important decisions and legal cases in the data protection field originated from Sweden.

Although digitization and the complex handling of cookie issues seem to have led to a weakening of this principled approach, it is undeniable that Sweden has played a significant role historically in shaping data protection in Europe. And

---

published as a doctoral thesis, University of Gothenburg, 1999. Lödén discusses how Sweden's neutrality during the war and its subsequent role as "moral conscience" can be seen as strategies for managing the country's complex position in post-war international politics.

[24] Lee, Miles, *Sweden and European Integration* (1997).

Sweden today, unlike Denmark, can boast a series of high-profile regulatory decisions with substantial penalty amounts.

"Never again"

In 2024, Sweden joined the North Atlantic Treaty Organization (NATO) after much, extensive hemming and hawing. In doing so, the country did not just say goodbye to the situational neutrality policy that had been part of Swedish security policy for 200 years—it definitively closed the door on the military non-alignment and neutrality that had characterized Sweden since World War II and the Cold War.

How NATO membership will affect Sweden's national self-image in the long term and its approach to interstate and international relations, remains to be seen. It will be what you make of it, as they say.

It is also easy for me to judge, with hindsight, the mistakes and difficult political decisions that Sweden made during the 1930s and 40s, and during the Cold War. (And to forget how right Sweden was with the Data Act in the 1970s.) It is also easy to give solemn memorial speeches on the theme of "Never again." Much harder it is building and maintaining a stronger immune response for democracy. But with the General Data Protection Regulation—the GDPR—we Europeans have remarkably successfully managed to find an important vaccine against tyranny. We put this in place, because we have the benefit of hindsight.

It is incumbent upon us to live up to it.

It is also a beautiful legislation—built on and anchored in human rights, as formulated in the European Union's Charter of Fundamental Rights.

I call it legal poetry.

II

The Laws

4. What is personal data?

For someone like me who lacks a photographic memory and considers herself reasonably intelligent (I hope), it was not until I began reflecting on the concept of privacy and understanding the connection between my right to protect my privacy and my personal data that GDPR transformed from an abstract bureaucratic acronym coined by EU "technocrats" into sensible regulation rooted in fundamental human rights.

This is something every company, organization, and individual should want to stand behind. Especially if you work on or with the web, since technological development is racing ahead and offering countless opportunities to raise a cautionary GDPR finger. But also because new sister regulations have emerged on extremely necessary grounds to complement and reshape the playing field for digital marketing and everything else IT-related in various ways. (Did someone say AI Act?)

But the step from thinking the General Data Protection Regulation is reasonable to understanding what it actually requires, can feel enormous. GDPR is not exactly light reading. After all, it consists of 99 articles and 173 so-called recitals. But it is not impossible—it may even be enjoyable if you break it down in an understandable way.

So, let us start from the ground up, beginning with the lowest common denominator or most fundamental building block of the GDPR—the concept of personal data.

To be or not to be personal data

Say you have a piece of information—it could be text, an image, or something else entirely, like a blood sample or a fingerprint. How do you know if this information qualifies as personal data, by definition?

GDPR's answer here is basically "it depends."

According to the regulation, the same information can be personal data in one context but not in another. What determines this is whether the information can be linked to a person—an identifiable person. The simplest way to explain this is with a first name like Anna. There are quite a few people named Anna in the world, so if you are standing in front of a large group of people, the data point "Anna" tells you very little about who you are talking about. But if you also know that Anna is the CEO of a large, well-known company, it suddenly becomes a piece of information that allows you to identify Anna.

Another example is a human arm with a uniquely designed tattoo. If the arm did not have a tattoo, or any other physical identification, it would "just" be an arm. But with the tattoo, the arm becomes personal data. The same thing if you could extract biometric data from the arm, such as through a blood sample that could be used to identify who the arm belongs to.

But often, it is more straightforward.

Take a license plate number, for example. Even though it is primarily personal data for a country's vehicle registration authority, anyone who sees and writes down a license plate number can—through that authority—look up who owns the vehicle.

The same applies to a blood sample. Since it contains DNA that can theoretically always be linked to a specific person, it is also always personal data, as long as the sample still exists and has not been destroyed.

Note that GDPR allows individual member states to determine whether information on a deceased person is personal data. Denmark has chosen to do this, which means your personal data is still protected by the legislation after you have left this earthly life—at least for ten years. This principle is convoluted when it comes to historically significant individuals, for whom the public interest in preserving or using information for, say, social science research may conflict with the deceased's or their survivors' right to preserve the privacy of the deceased. In such cases, the public interest in information access may outweigh privacy protection—this is an assessment that must be made case by case.

Of the 99 articles of the GDPR, it is Article 4 (Section 1) that clarifies what *personal data* actually is. The legal text states that "any information" relating to an "identified or identifiable natural person" constitutes personal data. This means personal data can be absolutely anything—an image, an audio file, text, a number—IF it can be linked to a living person.

But how then, do you know if a person is "identifiable"?

The answer is that this may happen in two ways: directly or indirectly. Directly through something like a name, social security number, or passport number. Indirectly by piecing together different bits of information that together make it possible to identify someone. And to help us along Article 4(1) mentions several categories, such as location data and online identifiers. In plain language, these can include items like:

- o   Where the person is located
- o   Various numbers and codes used online
- o   How the person looks or feels
- o   The person's genes
- o   How the person thinks and feels mentally
- o   The person's finances
- o   The person's cultural background
- o   How the person lives and behaves

The beauty of how Article 4 defines the concept is that it does so in a technology-neutral way: It works equally well for ordinary personal data in a physical document, like names and addresses, as it does for the more modern digital traces, we as individuals leave behind on the web, for example.

Compare it to when you visit an online store where you look at a pair of red shoes. If the store owners want to show you ads for those shoes when you later browse other websites (subjecting you to what is called retargeting), the store needs to know that you are you, so to speak. It does this by assigning you (essentially your browser) a unique code—a so-called cookie ID.

The code itself is a random collection of characters, but because it can be linked to your browsing behavior, which products you have looked at, when you are typically active online, and maybe even where you are in the physical world, it becomes personal data.

The definition of personal data in Article 4 is fairly straightforward and transparent. At least in theory. In practice, however, many legal experts in the field have had to choose their words carefully when trying to figure out whether a piece of information constitutes personal data or not. Take an IP address, for example. To an IT technician, it is just a number combination that identifies a device on the web. But since the same IP address is often used by the same person, and since the internet service provider can link the address to a specific customer, it becomes personal data. But what happens if the IP address is shared by all employees at a company? Or if it changes every time someone connects?

Danish lawyer and researcher Kasper Bjerre Hendrup Andersen has done quite the heavy lifting in this area by studying how the concept of personal data is actually used in practice, both by companies and in courts, to create a clear framework for anyone who sometimes feels confused by the personal data concept in their daily work.

Andersen's research demonstrates that when determining whether something is personal data or not, it is usually enough to focus on two things: Is there a connection between the information and a person, and can that person be identified? It may sound obvious, but it makes it much easier to assess whether something you are dealing with is or is not personal data, in context, so to speak.

Let us take the IP address as an example again. The connection to a person exists—after all, someone is using the IP address. (Andersen calls this the relationship requirement). But is the person identifiable? (Andersen calls this the identification requirement). Yes, usually, through the internet service provider. That is why an IP address can be personal data, even though it is technically just a number combination. Note, however, that it is important to distinguish between a static IP address and a dynamic IP address. The static one can identify the device permanently and thus the person using the device. But with dynamic addresses, it depends, again, since the internet service provider can regularly change the IP address. That is why the Court of Justice of the European Union has established that even dynamic IP addresses can constitute personal data, but only if there are legal means to link the address to an identifiable person, for example by requesting additional information from the internet service provider.[25]

But what happens if we take another digital tracking method, like counting how many times someone clicks a button on a webpage? There is indeed a connection to a person (after all, someone is clicking), but if the clicks are recorded completely anonymously without any connection to a specific visitor, then the person is not identifiable and therefore it is not personal data.

In other words, Andersen gives the data protection world two handrails, one on each side of the GDPR staircase, that you can hold onto. Because his research shows that even though Article 4(1) contains four components, in practice mainly two questions are needed to be asked about the information you have at hand:

1. Is there a connection between the information and a person?
2. Can that person be identified, directly or indirectly, with the help of the information?

---

[25] CJEU, Case C-582/14, Patrick Breyer v Bundesrepublik Deutschland, Judgment of 19 October 2016. See also GDPRhub, CJEU - C-582/14 – Breyer.

If the answer is yes to both these questions, we can with great certainty say "yes, this is personal data."

When personal data becomes extra sensitive

Once you have determined whether what you are dealing with is personal data or not, you also need to be aware of whether it additionally involves "sensitive personal data." There is an entire article in the GDPR, Article 9, which breaks down what the legislators mean by this. But it does not actually say "sensitive" in Article 9—instead, it is called "special categories" of personal data.

And even in this area, you do not need to complicate things unless the circumstances require some extra thought. Most people intuitively understand that personal data revealing something about one's health or religion is extra "sensitive." But if you are feeling uncertain, Article 9 lists 8 categories of personal data that require extra care:

- o Your ethnic background
- o Your political opinions
- o Your religion
- o Your trade union membership
- o Your genetic information
- o Your health
- o Your sex life or sexual orientation
- o Your biometric data that can identify you (like fingerprints or facial recognition)

The point of Article 9 is to clarify that the GDPR has strict requirements for handling personal data of this nature. The main rule is that it is prohibited to process them unless you have a particular exception.

In other words, it is not particularly easy to get permission to use sensitive personal data for marketing purposes. It can be allowed, but only if explicit consent has been obtained from the data subject. This consent requirement is stricter than for processing ordinary personal data. It is important to remember that regardless of whether you are processing ordinary or sensitive personal data, you must always follow the fundamental principles in Article 5 of the GDPR. (One of these principles is purpose limitation—that personal data may only be collected for specific, explicitly stated, and legitimate purposes.)

When it comes to sensitive personal data, you therefore face a double challenge: First, you must have a specific lawful basis under Article 9 of the GDPR (which for marketing usually means explicit consent), and second, just as with processing all personal data, you must follow the fundamental principles in Article 5[26].

An example of this is when you own a gym and want to send targeted ads to people with certain health problems. The question you need to ask yourself here is whether you think it is worth it. You need to be very careful about how you collect informed consent for this, and how you store and process this information securely. Do you even risk coming across as a bit too intrusive toward your target audience?

Note, however, that Article 9 has several other exceptions you can rely on if you want to handle sensitive personal data. But for someone working in marketing, it is primarily consent that is relevant.

From a digital marketing perspective, you need to be very aware of how ordinary personal data can be "transformed" into sensitive data. For example, if you track and identify people who visit your website using a web analytics tool like Google Analytics, this happens by giving each visitor a client ID via a cookie. There is nothing unusual about that, although it still

---

[26] I make these principles easier to understand from a marketing perspective in Chapter 19.

47

needs to be done in compliance with privacy regulations. But if your website is about healthcare, and you collect information about how each client ID repeatedly visits specific pages for particular diseases through web analytics, you can indirectly end up processing sensitive personal data about the visitor's health through this tracking. Or worse, end up sending that data to a third party, and/or to a third party in a country outside the EU/EEC that is deemed unsafe (i.e., lacks an adequacy decision) by the EU to transfer personal data without certain guard rails. That is why many organizations handling health-related information choose more privacy-focused web analytics tools, like Fathom or Piwik Pro. Some of the advantages of such tools are that they sometimes allow you to host all analytics data on your own servers and thereby retain full control over the information. This also means you avoid sharing your visitors' data with a large tech company, which could then use the information for their own purposes.

As a website owner, you may have a legitimate interest in understanding how visitors use your health-related website. You might want to optimize content, improve navigation, or see which health topics engage the most. But two problems arise here.

First, you are processing sensitive personal data about health, which requires specific, explicit consent from the visitor. This means the ordinary cookie banner is not sufficient, since Article 9 requires explicit consent for processing sensitive personal data.[27]

Second, if you use Google Analytics, you are sharing these sensitive personal data with Google. Even if you had the visitor's explicit consent to collect the data, you must be certain that Google has the right to receive and process them as well. This becomes particularly problematic since Google may use Analytics data for its own purposes, and once data has reached Google, you have limited control over how it is used.

---

[27] See more about the cookie banner issue in the book's third part.

Another scenario is running a website with different types of content, and you use a CRM system that links a user's email address with their browsing behavior on your site. If the user regularly reads articles about a certain political orientation, and you save this information linked to the user, you have potentially created information about the person's political opinions, and this is sensitive personal data.

What is important here is that it is the actual connection between the identifier (client ID, email address, etc.) and the behavior that can create sensitive personal data, especially if you build up and store profiles over time.

When it comes to handling sensitive personal data, it is important to be aware of the requirement in the GDPR (Article 35) for a so-called Data Protection Impact. This does not mean you always have to conduct such an assessment. An DPIA is required specifically in situations where the processing is likely to result in a high risk to individuals' rights and freedoms.

When personal data become anonymous, or nearly anonymous

In 2006, Netflix released an anonymous database containing 100 million movie ratings from its users. The purpose was to create a competition in which programmers could use the data to develop a better recommendation system. Whoever managed to improve the system by 10 percent would win $1 million. Netflix was careful to remove all personal information—no names, no email addresses, just anonymous ID numbers and the ratings each user had given to different movies.

But it did not take long before researchers discovered they could identify individual Netflix users by comparing the "anonymous" ratings with public reviews on IMDb. By matching just a handful of movie ratings with timestamps, they could identify specific people in the "anonymous" database with high confidence. Suddenly, the anonymous movie preferences were not so anonymous anymore.

This is a particularly illuminating example of why anonymizing personal data is often much harder than you might initially think. Simply removing names and other obvious identifiers is rarely sufficient. But fear not—the General Data Protection Regulation provides substantial guidance here. First, the GDPR clarifies that you must distinguish between hiding personal data and truly getting rid of it. The latter is the gold standard if you want to be completely in the clear, and that is how the GDPR defines anonymization. The former, however, is called pseudonymization and means the data are merely hidden.

Pseudonymization is like putting the data in a box and keeping the key to that box. If you have a customer database where you replace all email addresses with random codes but maintain a separate list showing which code corresponds to which email address, then you have pseudonymized the data. This means it is still, by definition, personal data and must be handled in accordance with the GDPR.

With anonymization, however, you throw the key into the fires of Mount Doom. In other words, you have removed all possibilities of linking the information in question to a specific person. If you do this correctly, the data is no longer considered personal data and therefore falls outside the scope of the GDPR.

Unsurprisingly, truly anonymizing personal data is not particularly straightforward. Even if you remove all obvious identifiers like names, social security numbers, and addresses, the combination of remaining information can often still be used to identify individuals. For example, if you remove names and addresses from your customer or visitor data but keep zip codes, ages, and purchase history, that might be enough to identify specific people—especially when combined with other available data sources.

This is precisely what Netflix experienced when two researchers from the University of Texas, Arvind Narayanan and Vitaly Shmatikov, demonstrated how users in the Netflix dataset could be de-anonymized by correlating it with public reviews on IMDb. They could identify individual Netflix users with high confidence by matching as few as 8 movie ratings with dates.

The Netflix case was an American matter that led to a class action lawsuit against the company, resulting in Netflix canceling plans for a follow-up competition in 2010. Years later, when the GDPR came into effect in 2018, this case had already become a cautionary tale about the challenges of true anonymization.

And please keep in mind how easily we view the GDPR solely through the lens of our digitized existence. Remember that the regulation governs how you and I may handle personal data—regardless of what technology is used to collect, store, and process that data. So, it does not matter whether you handle personal data on paper or as ones and zeros—the regulation governs THAT you handle personal data.

With that said, let us take a closer look at the GDPR from a marketing perspective.

5. GDPR explained for marketers

I've developed a model—or process—to make it easier to put on your data protection hat or strap on your GDPR backpack in your daily work as a marketer. I'll walk you through this Privacy-First model in Chapter 19. In this chapter, however, you will get a more fundamental ABC rundown of what is what in the GDPR landscape.

In 2018, when the GDPR appeared like a stop sign on the information superhighway, everyone in marketing was forced to at least consider pumping the brakes. Mantras like "if you are not paying for the product, you are the product" became harder to ignore. And while it took time for skeptics like me to have that lightbulb moment, every company became legally obligated to review how they collect, process, and store personal data—from leads and customers, for instance. The law had teeth because the penalty fees were substantial and responsibility fell to a central authority in each country.

But what does this mean in practical terms? What do I, as a marketer, need to understand to comply with the legal requirements?

Before we unpack these questions, let me quietly note that not everything in this world revolves around marketing—the GDPR covers all industries and contexts. It is also easy to drown in the 99 articles and 173 recitals in the GDPR. The purpose of this book in general, and this chapter in particular, is to keep you from drowning. My hope is that it will feel more like flying. And since it is (probably) easier to take off when you are not too weighed down, here's the GDPR broken into nine bite-sized portions, perfectly portioned for the marketer's palate—a complete food pyramid for anyone who wants to understand what you need to know about the General Data Protection Regulation to respect both your business goals and your customers' and leads' privacy.

Nine things every marketer needs to know about the GDPR

1. Understand what constitutes personal data in your work
As the previous chapter indicates, you need to grab the bull by the horns and realize that whenever you send a newsletter, track visitors on your website, or run an advertising campaign on Facebook, you are collecting, sharing, and handling personal data. And by personal data, we do not just mean names and email addresses. A cookie ID that follows someone across different pages can be personal data. So can information about which products a particular visitor viewed in your online store.

2. Understand what is required to be allowed to use personal data in your work
To be permitted to use personal data, you must have a lawful basis to rely on, as data protection lawyers like to say. What they mean is that the GDPR gives you six possible grounds or reasons you can choose from to justify your right to process personal data. The key point is that you should have thought things through before you start collecting and processing data, so you know why you want to do something before you do it.

In reality, you as a marketer can mainly choose between two of the six lawful bases: consent and legitimate interests. Consent means that a person has said "yes" when you asked if you could use their personal data for a specific purpose. It must be a genuine "yes"— like when you ask a friend if you can borrow their car:

- o You cannot just take the keys and leave a note saying, "I assume it is okay" (it must be freely given and clear)
- o You cannot borrow the car for a quick trip around town and then drive it to another state (it must be specific to the purpose)

- You must explain why you want to borrow the car, for how long, and if there is anything else relevant (the person should understand what you mean by "borrowing the car")
- And your friend should be able to call anytime and ask you to bring the car back (consent should be as easy to withdraw as it is to give).

Legitimate interests can[28] be an alternative (though rarely), at least when it involves your customers. Imagine you run a bike shop and want to send an email to your customers about spring tune-up time. You sold each bike, you know when it was purchased, and you know when it needs servicing. Here you can argue that you have a legitimate interest in contacting each customer—it is in both the customer's and your interest that the bike functions properly. But if you instead wanted to send advertising about a completely new bike to the same customer, the threshold is higher and consent is a more sustainable path to take.

Note that you cannot mix consent for different purposes. If a lead has given you permission to send newsletters to them, you cannot automatically use the customer's data for targeted advertising or share it with a third party. Each new use of the personal data requires specific consent for that purpose (or another valid lawful basis).[29]

---

[28] At least from a Swedish perspective, due to how the Swedish Marketing Act is structured. It should be noted, however, that legitimate interests under the GDPR requires a careful assessment of each individual case, including the necessity test and balancing test (Recital 47 in GDPR). Even though the Marketing Act allows for the use of legitimate interests, consent is the main rule—both from an ePrivacy perspective and a data protection perspective. Direct marketing can be considered a legitimate interest under certain circumstances, but it requires that the processing be proportionate and expected by the data subject.

[29] Beware that public authorities may process personal data for statistical or research purposes under different lawful bases, such as public interest or legal obligation, and may not always require new, specific consent for each use. So,

3. Be transparent about what you do

Let us say you run an online store selling handmade jewelry. You collect email addresses to send out your newsletter, use cookies to track visitors, and share data with Facebook to enable targeted advertising. You must disclose all of this—not hidden in fine print at the bottom of the page—but clearly and accessibly. So skip the legalese. Instead of writing "The data controller processes personal data in accordance with..." it is better to go with "We at Anna's Jewelry collect your email address to..." Use this rule of thumb: If my grandfather wouldn't understand what I mean, I need to rephrase it.

Most companies choose to meet transparency requirements by linking to a privacy policy. Note, however, that the GDPR does not say you must write a privacy policy. The only thing the GDPR emphasizes in Articles 13(1) and 14(1) is that you, as the data controller, must provide information to the data subject at the time of collection. Linking to a privacy policy has become a practical way to fulfill transparency requirements. So a privacy policy does not need to look like a white document with straight text—format-wise.[30]

And as mentioned, a privacy policy should not be a legal dissertation. It should tell your visitors, customers, and leads:

- who is behind the policy and their contact details
- contact details to the Data Protection Officer (if there is one)
- what data you collect
- why you collect it
- what you use it for
- who you share it with

---

the requirements for lawful processing can differ depending on the context and the nature of the organization.

[30] Please note that a privacy policy describes how all personal data is handled, while a cookie policy specifically explains the use of cookies and similar technologies on your website.

- o how long you keep it
- o how they can exercise their rights

In addition, remember that transparency is good business. The simpler and more digestible your information is, the better it is for the reader. It also builds trust. Customers and followers appreciate honesty and clarity.

And for the curious: Transparency and information requirements can be found in Articles 12–14 of the GDPR. But remember—what matters is not the paragraphs, but that your customers understand what you do with their data. Think logically.

4. Customers, leads, and their rights

As a marketer, you probably sit on a list of personal data in, for example, your CRM system. A goldmine. But the gold is only on loan. Because the GDPR provides those whom the personal data concerns, a number of rights that you are obligated to respect:

The right to information
"What are you doing with my data?"

A customer should never have to guess what you do with their data. If you collect email addresses for newsletters, use cookies to track behavior on your website,[31] or share data with Facebook for advertising—tell them about it.

The right of access
"Show me everything you have about me."

When someone asks, you must be able to show what data you have collected. This means you need to know where all the different types of personal data are located.

---

[31] And when it comes to tracking and surveillance with cookies, the ePrivacy directive overlaps with the GDPR.

The right to rectification
"You have incorrect information about me."

When a customer moves or changes their last name, they should easily be able to get their information updated. Make sure you can update data in all systems where it exists. This requirement for updated information applies regardless of whether the affected individuals request it or not.

The right to erasure
Delete all my information."

When someone wants to be "forgotten," you must be able to erase their data from all systems. Yes, even that valuable purchase history and those finely segmented customer profiles. But this right is not absolute—if you as the data controller have another lawful basis to process the personal data in question, you may have the right to continue doing so, despite the data subject's wishes.

The right to restriction
"Stop all use of my data for now"

A customer can request that you temporarily stop using their data, for example if they suspect something is wrong. You must be able to suspend the use at least temporarily without deleting the data.

The right to data portability
"I want my data in a usable format."

If you have collected personal data directly from the customer and process it digitally (like when someone fills out a form or creates a profile on your site), they should be able to get the data in a reusable format. For example, someone who registered for your newsletter, should be able to get their contact information and preferences in a structured format like CSV or JSON.

This right is more powerful than it might first appear. Take Facebook, for example: You can contact Meta and request all the data they have about you in a structured, machine-readable format, even if that means years of posts, likes, searches, ad interactions, location data, and countless other data points that build up your digital footprint. Austrian privacy activist Max Schrems famously did exactly this in 2011, receiving 1,200 pages of personal data from Facebook, including information he thought he had deleted.

For your business or site, this means that whether someone filled out a simple newsletter form on your site or created a detailed customer profile, they have the right to get their contact information, preferences, and other data in structured format.

The right to object
"Stop sending me advertising."

This is especially important for marketers: When someone says no to your marketing, you must respect it. Immediately. No "but" or "maybe later."

The right not to be subject to automated decision-making
"I do not want to be judged by a machine."

If you use systems that automatically make decisions about people (like adjusting prices or denying someone membership), they have the right to have the decision reviewed by a human. For example, if a bank uses an algorithm to automatically approve or deny loan applications, the applicant has the right to request a human review of the decision.

Always be ready!
Service-mindedness is crucial when someone wants to exercise their rights. Therefore, you need to have:

o   A clear process—who does what when a request comes in?

- o Quick handling—no longer than a month, can be extended to three months if needed.
- o Documentation—save requests and your responses.
- o Trained staff—everyone on the team needs to understand the basics.

Let me give you a tip here: There are software solutions that can automate this for you, so you can receive, verify, and handle requests without turning your entire organization upside down.

5. Do not collect more than you need

Just because you can collect data does not mean you should. Less is often much more, because the GDPR contains a very important principle called data minimization.

Imagine you have a form on your website where visitors can sign up to receive newsletters. Asking for an email address feels obvious. But do you also need to know when the person's birthday is, their phone number, and marital status?

Every extra piece of data you collect:

- o Increases your risk in the event of a data breach
- o Makes it more complicated to keep the information updated
- o Can scare away potential subscribers
- o Costs money to store and manage

For example, if you run an online store, you need a delivery address for physical products. But for digital products, email is sufficient. Asking for a delivery address in that case violates the data minimization principle. Ask yourself: Can I achieve my goal with less data? If the answer is yes, you should collect less data.

A current example is a decision from the Court of Justice of the European Union that established it is not necessary to collect information about gender (e.g., "Mr." or "Mrs.") when purchasing train tickets, since this is not relevant to the purpose.[32]

6. Only use data for what you said you would
Say you have an online store where you sell sportswear and exercise equipment. A customer gives you their email address to receive order confirmations and delivery information. After a while, the marketing team realizes it would be perfect to send customized workout recommendations to all customers, based on their purchase history.

Is this permitted? No, not without consent.

Or say you have a list of subscribers to your newsletter about gardening. Your friend starts a company selling garden furniture and asks if you can share your email list with him.

Is this permitted? No, because the subscribers did not consent to that. Always treat personal data as a loan. When someone lends you their email address to receive your newsletter, they are lending it to receive your newsletter—for nothing else. If you want to do something more with the email address, you must ask for permission first.

7. Protect data you collect
Personal data must be protected, both technically and organizationally. One way to enhance security is to use pseudonymization (see Chapter 4). Instead of seeing "anna.andersson@mail.com bought running shoes," you see "user A12B3 bought running shoes." This reduces the risk if data falls into the wrong hands.

But security is about more than just technical solutions. You also need to keep track of:

- o Who has access to the personal data
- o How long the data is stored

---

[32] See Court of Justice of the European Union judgment of January 9, 2025, in Case C-394/23: https://eur-lex.europa.eu/legal-content/EN/TXT/?uri=celex:62023CJ0394

o   How the data is protected when shared with others
o   How you detect and handle potential data breaches

It is also important to note that security is particularly critical when it comes to outsourcing data processing. When you engage a data processor[33] to handle personal data on your behalf, you must ensure they meet the security requirements of the GDPR. This means:

o   You must enter into a written agreement (data processing agreement) with the processor that instructs the data processor and specifies security requirements.
o   You should regularly review and evaluate the security measures of the processor
o   You must ensure the processor only processes data according to your instructions
o   You should have a plan for how data will be handled if the collaboration with the processor ends. Should the data be given back or deleted?

The GDPR is clear about security requirements. It asks you to be vigilant and aware, while also stating that what is appropriate depends on what type of data you handle and what risks exist. The more sensitive the data, the higher the security requirements, for example.

Data protection and cybersecurity are really two sides of the same coin. A data breach, for example, means that personal data has been accidentally or unlawfully destroyed, lost, changed, disclosed, or accessed by someone who should not have access. This makes a data breach not only a security problem but also a

---

[33] It is important to understand the difference between a data controller and a data processor under the GDPR. When a data controller engages a third party to process personal data on its behalf (a data processor), the controller must ensure that the processor complies with GDPR requirements. This includes entering into a written data processing agreement in accordance with Article 28 of the GDPR and assessing the risks of any potential transfers of personal data to third countries.

threat to people's right to privacy. And conversely, by protecting personal data, you simultaneously build stronger defenses against cyberattacks. That is why security is a cornerstone of all data protection work, whether you handle data internally or outsource processing to a third party, such as MailChimp or Amazon Web Services.

8. Do you need a Data Protection Officer?
A data protection officer might sound like a role only large companies need, but even smaller operations may need to appoint one. It does not depend on the size of the company but on what you do with the personal data.

As a marketer, you primarily need to consider whether your company monitors people regularly and systematically on a large scale. That might sound alarming, but in practice it is about extensive tracking of visitors to your website, large scale profiling for targeted marketing, or the like.

What is "large scale"? If you run a small e-commerce business that sends newsletters to a few thousand customers, it usually does not count as large scale. But if you run an advertising platform that tracks millions of users across the entire web, then you are definitely in large-scale territory.

If you collect particularly sensitive data such as health information or political opinions, you also need a data protection officer. But for most marketers, this is rarely relevant—we usually stick to less sensitive items like email addresses and purchase history.

Are you unsure? Talk to a lawyer or contact the Data Protection Authority in your country. Better be safe than sorry.

9. When personal data cross jurisdictional boundaries
As a marketer, you use various digital tools for analytics, email campaigns, and advertising. Many of these services are operated by companies that act as data processors, which means they process personal data on your behalf according to your

instructions. Examples of such services include cloud service providers or analytics tools that handle customer data.

It is important to understand that when you engage a data processor based outside the EU/EEA, personal data may be transferred to and processed in a country that does not provide an adequate level of data protection under EU law. The risk exists even if the data is physically stored within the EU, because the company operating the service may be subject to the laws of its home country, which could require it to disclose personal data to local authorities. Therefore, controllers must carefully assess and ensure appropriate safeguards are in place to protect the data and comply with GDPR requirements.

For certain countries outside the EU/EEA, the European Commission has decided that the country's data protection level is sufficiently high. This is called an adequacy decision and means that transfer of personal data to these countries is permitted without special conditions. For other countries, however, additional safeguards are required, such as standard contractual clauses or binding corporate rules.

You should exercise due diligence when choosing services and tools for your marketing. And this applies to all aspects of the requirements of the GDPR, not just when dealing with companies based in third countries. So, if a service turns out to be non-compliant, find one that is.

Wrapping up. As marketers, we have gotten used to using various digital services that we integrate with our website or online store, such as social media and web analytics tools. We often do not think about the fact that these tools or products collect personal data or information that, indirectly and combined with other data, can identify a human being.

The nine bite-sized pieces above give you as a marketer a solid foundation when it comes to the GDPR. But they are naturally not exhaustive. The GDPR contains, as mentioned, 99 articles and many more details than we can cover here. But hopefully it feels a bit more manageable. Now, let's take a closer look at GDPR's little sister.

6. The lives of others

The ePrivacy Directive is so much more than a cookie law.

The Academy Award-winning film *The Lives of Others* takes place in East Berlin, in the German Democratic Republic, during the 1980s. Stasi agent Gerd Wiesler employs a range of advanced surveillance techniques to spy on a prominent playwright and his partner. This means the couple's apartment is bugged; Wiesler uses headphones and recording equipment to document the pair's conversations, and he taps into their phone line to listen to all incoming and outgoing calls. Wiesler finds no evidence of disloyalty. When his superiors ask him to fabricate evidence against the playwright, Wiesler faces a moral dilemma and begins questioning his role and the system he serves.

The film is gripping because the Stasi agent cannot confide his thoughts and feelings to anyone. The situation illuminates not only what it means to be unable to think or express oneself freely in human relationships and constantly fearing surveillance, it also serves as a reminder of people's inner strength and integrity, and a critique of the methods that can be used to control and constrain us.

Through Wiesler's use of surveillance equipment, the film demonstrates how technical tools can be used to deprive people of their right to privacy. And it is precisely this aspect— protection against actual technical surveillance—that the ePrivacy Directive addresses and attempts to regulate. In short, it is a directive that the EU adopted in 2002 as an important complement to the predecessor of the GDPR—the Data Protection Directive[34].

It took me several attempts before I began to grasp the ePrivacy Directive. Like others, I fixated on the GDPR and its

---

34 Yes, Sweden's Personal Data Act (PuL) was Sweden's implementation of EU Data Protection Directive 95/46/EC.

significance for me as a marketer. Perhaps that is not surprising, since the GDPR is a regulation and therefore carries different weight than an EU directive. But the ePrivacy Directive is by no means an insignificant legislation. Indeed, quite the contrary.

The right to think freely vs. freedom of speech

The predecessor to the ePrivacy Directive (Directive 97/66/EC) was adopted as early as 1997, resting on the same original intent as the 1995 Data Protection Directive (the predecessor of the GDPR): to protect fundamental human rights in the digital era. However, while the predecessor targeted the telecommunications sector specifically, the new ePrivacy directive, from 2002, had an expanded scope that addressed electronic communication. In 2009 the ePrivacy directive was updated, and it remains, in practice, a crucial complement to the General Data Protection Regulation to this day. They are like legal siblings—little sister and big sister.

I also find it interesting that both the ePrivacy Directive and the original Data Protection Directive are said to have their origins in the same 1990 document, but for political reasons they were split into two separate regulatory frameworks. This division reflects two different aspects of protection: personal data on one hand and confidential communication on the other—a distinction with roots stretching back to the lessons learned from the Nazi surveillance state discussed in Chapter 3.

However, even though the ePrivacy Directive can be considered the GDPR's little sister, it does not mean the GDPR always takes precedence if the two should clash. The reason for this is that the directive is what is called "lex specialis" (the special legislation) in legal terms, while the GDPR is "lex generalis" (the general legislation). In other words, if the directive explicitly has something more specific to say about a matter that the GDPR does not address in as much detail, then the directive's rules apply.

For example, if a website wanted to use cookies to track and profile its visitors, they might (possibly) have been able to rely on the GDPR and the legitimate interest basis to get permission to do this. But since little sister specialis says that cookies and tracking require consent, it is the stricter requirements of the directive that apply. The website must therefore ALWAYS ensure they have obtained the visitor's active "yes, please" (unless we are talking about strictly necessary cookies). But note that little sister and big sister hold hands here, since the directive refers to the GDPR for more information regarding what constitutes consent.

The most obvious reason these two laws work so well together is that little sister and big sister lean on and protect the same fundamental values regarding people's right to privacy and personal integrity. But while big sister focuses on data in the form of personal information, little sister is sharp on the broader concept of electronic communication—that is, people's right to confidentiality in electronic communication. It explicitly illegalizes engagement in what the Stasi agents did during the GDR-era.

Also note the word confidentiality, which is central to the ePrivacy Directive. It is actually a complex concept that encompasses not just your right to your data or personal information, but also your right to express yourself and communicate freely when you speak on the phone, send an email, a text message, and so on. In other words, the directive protects your right to think freely in a way that a Stasi agent like Wiesler could not.

Here too, it took me several attempts before the penny dropped, because thinking freely is not the same thing as freedom of speech. Are you with me on this?

Here is my explanation:

The right to think freely and to discuss thoughts in confidentiality is a fundamental aspect of personal integrity protected by the ePrivacy Directive. This directive ensures that you and your friends or acquaintances can talk and write to each other electronically—for example, over the phone or computer—without some outsider trying to eavesdrop or influence you. The personal sphere is in focus here.

This right should NOT be confused with freedom of speech, which in democratic societies is typically protected by constitutional provisions. This right encompasses our right to express ourselves publicly—for example, by voicing opinions in speech, writing, or images.

I think it is important to take the time to understand this distinction because it helps us not mixing apples and oranges when discussing social media from both societal and marketing perspectives.

For example, when someone criticizes a social network for moderating or removing certain types of posts, we talk about freedom of speech in the public square—they are the oranges. But the same platform can simultaneously be criticized for reading private messages and monitoring every activity a person does on the platform and across other domains outside the platform in order to target ads more effectively and curate the feed to keep that person scrolling for a longer stretch of time. This concerns the right to confidential communication—they are the apples.

By making a distinction between these perspectives, it becomes easier to have more constructive discussions about how we as citizens and marketers can best protect and safeguard different types of fundamental rights on the web and elsewhere.

But what about the cookie question?

The ePrivacy Directive is often called the "Cookie Directive" or "cookie law" because of its 2009 update, which took effect in May 2011. This update clarified that cookies and other tracking technologies cannot be placed on a user's device—such as Safari, Firefox, or Chrome browsers—without the user's prior consent. In other words, before this change, users typically had to opt out if they did not want to be tracked; after the change, users must opt in by actively giving their consent before any tracking occurs. But that is not how it reads in the legal text, which instead refers to terminal equipment—a broader concept, which today also encompasses mobile apps, cars, Internet of Things (IoT) devices, and more. Hence the concept of terminal equipment is crucial for understanding the scope of the directive in today's digital landscape.

In the film, we see how Stasi agent Wiesler wiretaps the playwright couple's phone line and installs microphones in their home. Back then, physical access to the residence and telephone lines was required to surveil people. Today, we carry or own devices that can be monitored remotely: our cell phones, smart TVs, and connected cars. All of these are examples of terminal equipment covered by the directive, and which need protection from surveillance.

When you install an app on your cell phone, for example, it is possible for it to collect information about you. It might want access to your location data, your contacts, your photos. But unlike Wiesler's microphones, which were physically tangible items, today's digital surveillance is often invisible to the user. This can happen through third-party components built into the app, through various forms of digital tracking, or by the app collecting information about your usage patterns. All of this represents ways in which information is stored or retrieved from your terminal equipment, and is therefore covered by the consent requirements of the directive. Yet we do not see consent requests in apps to the same extent as we do on websites, though the situation is improving.

Note that the 2009 amendment also emphasized that consent is not necessary if the cookie in question is strictly necessary and solely for the service—such as a website—to function properly. (However, you must still inform users that you are using so called strictly necessary cookies.)

It is also important to note that while the ePrivacy Directive provides a common framework for all EU countries, each nation has slightly different ways of implementing and applying it.

This means that the way in which cookies are regulated may differ somewhat between EU countries.[35]

In Germany, for example, the directive has been incorporated into their Telecommunications-Telemedia-Data Protection Act (TTDPA). And in Sweden, the ePrivacy Directive has been implemented through the Electronic Communications Act (LEK). In Sweden, it is therefore the LEK that specifically safeguards personal data protection and privacy within electronic communications.

Denmark is particularly interesting because of how they have chosen to clarify what the "cookie" rules mean in practice. While the Swedish authority responsible for online tracking has long stayed vague on the subject, Denmark has been more decisive in that their GDPR-authority has developed guidelines for how companies should ask for permissions before collection information from users' devices. These guidelines emphasized, among other things, that it should be equally easy to say no as to say yes to cookies and tracking[36].

It may seem peculiar that it was the Danish GDPR-authority (Datatilsynet) and not the government entity which formally owned the online-tracking issue that created and published the guidelines. And it is. From a distance it looks like Datatilsynet could not accept that those who should inform, did nothing, and then they took it on themselves to clarify the rules. And recently the Danish government seem to have concluded that the responsibility for cookie rules in Denmark was misplaced and

---

[35] A regulation, like the GDPR, is a type of legislation that applies directly in all member countries immediately. A regulation does not need to be integrated into any existing national law. Also, a member country like Sweden cannot enact laws that contradict the regulation, and if it turns out that a member country has national legislation that conflicts with the regulation's provisions, the regulation takes precedence. The regulation should also be directly applied by national courts and other authorities.

36 These guidelines were published by Datatilsynet—despite responsibility at the time technically lying with the Danish Business Authority: Cookies and GDPR: https://www.datatilsynet.dk/regler-og-vejledning/gdpr-univers-for-smaa-virksomheder/cookies-og-gdpr

removed it from the Danish Business Authority to the Danish Agency for Digital Government, i.e. from *Erhvervsstyrelsen* to *Digitaliseringsstyrelsen*. This seems a wise decision. The latter continues the work of informing about the issue and monitoring compliance.[37]

Denmark being clearer and more active on the online-tracking issue can in part be explained by how Denmark gave the "cookie-part" of the ePrivacy Directive its own dedicated law explicitly called the "cookiebekendtgørelsen", instead of—like Sweden—simply letting it be an integrated part of a broader national electronic communications law. This emphasis on cookie regulations is not about Denmark making up their own rules, but about how they, as soon as the directive was updated in 2011, chose to clearly spell out what little sister (ePrivacy from the cookie perspective) means in practice; how it interacts with GDPR, and not least, why it is important that these rules are followed.

That said, from an oversight perspective, it is not ideal whether in Denmark or Sweden, that ePrivacy and GDPR are split between two different authorities.

In Norway, however, the situation is different today, as they enacted the "ekomloven"[38] at the end of 2024 and placed oversight responsibility under the Data Protection Authority. Thus, Norway has a situation where both confidentiality and tracking issues sit at the same table as data protection and privacy issues, which bodes well for strong enforcement operations. Does that mean the Norwegian Datatilsynet will leverage the situation accordingly? Well, when it comes to taking principled action on these questions, Norway has a strong track record. Their Datatilsynet has taken decisive steps against tech giants such as Meta, for example. In 2023, Datatilsynet imposed a temporary ban on Meta's use of

---

[37] Danish Agency for Digital Government, Cookie Guidelines:
https://digst.dk/tilsyn/sporingsteknologiomraadet/cookievejledningen/
[38] Electronic Communications Act (ekomloven), LOV-2024-12-13-76:
https://lovdata.no/dokument/NL/lov/2024−12−13−76

personal data for behavioral advertising on Facebook and Instagram, citing violations of the GDPR. The authority acted independently and swiftly, threatening significant daily fines and referring the matter to the European Data Protection Board to seek a broader, pan-European effect. This proactive enforcement approach has set Norway apart as one of the more assertive data protection regulators in Europe, signaling a willingness to prioritize user privacy even in the face of powerful international companies.

The GDPR & ePrivacy go hand in hand

The Danish approach to clarify how the GDPR and the ePrivacy intersect is reasonable because the ePrivacy Directive complements the General Data Protection Regulation, and both are rooted in the same fundamental human rights and freedoms, specifically:

o   The EU Charter of Fundamental Rights, and
o   The European Convention on Human Rights

To be super precise, we are talking about Articles 7 and 8 of the EU Charter and Article 8 of the European Convention. Together, these three articles establish that all people have the right to private life, family life, and confidential communication.

I cannot emphasize enough the importance of taking a deep breath and truly appreciate the significance of these charters and articles. Whenever you feel yourself getting tangled up in the details of various laws, it can be refreshing to step back to see the bigger picture. These documents remind us of what is ultimately at stake, and what legislators fundamentally aim to protect and prevent. Of course, the human rights referenced in these three articles are not the only human rights on which the EU's core documents are based. The right to privacy is not an absolute right. Be that as it may.

While Stasi agents had to physically install surveillance equipment in each apartment, today's digital technologies can collect data on millions of people simultaneously. Cookies, pixels, and server-side tracking[39] are today "legal" tools for data collection, if done properly. But since compliance remains relatively low in this area, we are still left with the follow-up questions and concerns about vigilance, which the story of Wiesler's wiretapping brings to mind:

Who has the right to know what about whom?

Surveillance capitalism

When the Data Protection Directive grew up to become the General Data Protection Regulation, the plan was for the ePrivacy Directive too to be transformed into a regulation. But that did not happen.

In this section, I will explore the limitations of the ePrivacy Directive and why it does not seem sufficient to protect online communication in the way legislators intended when it first took effect. To understand the essence of the ePrivacy Directive and its role on today's web, I spoke with Aurélis Pols, is a privacy engineer, DPO and ethics expert who has served as a board member of the European Centre for Privacy and Cybersecurity.[40]

---

[39]A pixel is like a tiny, invisible tracker that immediately sends information back to you about what someone does on your website (think of it as a "live report"). Cookies, on the other hand, are like small notes saved on the user's browser that may "remember," who they are when they come back to your site. Server-side tracking means your company's server processes and forwards visitor data, rather than relies only on what happens in the user's browser, giving you more control. For more in-depth information on the issue, see Chapter 7 "What is a Cookie?

40 Aurélie Pols has a background in econometrics, data governance and eBusiness. And at ECPC, based at Maastricht University, where she taught courses in the law program (LLM) and the Data Protection Officer Program. Throughout the years, Pols has collaborated with the European Commission on programs around ethics (for the EDPS), as technology expert (for the EDPB) and as an expert member of the Observatory for The Online Platform

Pols begins by strongly objecting to the directive being called "the cookie law."

"The cookie issue is just a small part of the directive", she says, confirming how the cookie focus first emerged when the directive received a minor update in 2009 (taking effect in 2011), which clarified that consent was required if you wanted cookies to be placed on a user's device, or "terminal equipment," as it is called in the law.

"The ePrivacy Directive is first and foremost a law about confidentiality in electronic communication", she emphasizes, pointing out that the directive should rather be viewed as a kind of anti-surveillance legislation, as it aims to protect individuals' electronic communication from unwanted eavesdropping, collection, and use of data without consent.

But because the law emerged in a different technological landscape than what exists today, it is struggling to keep up. To illustrate the situation, Pols provides an example.

"If you send a classic text message via your phone—that is, a text message that goes through your telephone operator—then the protection from surveillance is much stronger than when it happens through something like WhatsApp." "The directive today cannot safeguard privacy protection in the same way for OTT services", Pols explains. (See more on what OTT-services are in the next section.)

However, the situation is more complex than that. While WhatsApp and similar services are now covered by the regulations, they are treated differently than traditional telecom operators. In Sweden, for example, they do not need to register their operations with the Swedish Post and Telecom Authority

---

Economy. Pols is also an entrepreneur who co-founded and successfully sold her digital analytics agency back in 2008 before turning to privacy, to, as she expresses it, "supporting the values I cherishes within our increasingly digitalized and data driven societies". Today, she works full time as a Privacy Expert for EU based Amadeus, the world´s leading provider of travel technology. At Amadeus her focus lies with security functions and standardization of data exchanges within the travel sector.

(PTS) in the same way telecom companies must. In practice, this gives them greater leeway in how they handle user data.

App, app, app

OTT services stands for Over-The-Top services—essentially services that operate as a layer on top of "the network," as distinct from traditional telephony and mobile services, which are network services in themselves. OTT services can also be described as internet-based communication.

However, it is crucial to understand that OTT services encompass far more than just communication apps like WhatsApp and Microsoft Teams. Every app on your phone is essentially an OTT service. Your weather app, fitness tracker, games, social media apps, and so on—they are all OTT services, which collect and handle data in different ways and to varying degrees. This becomes particularly interesting when you consider how these apps actually function. Unlike a traditional telecom service such as a phone call, where the operator simply facilitates the conversation itself, a modern app can collect a vast array of different data types.

This becomes particularly clear when you examine how a mobile app operates. It is significantly more complex than a website when it comes to collecting and managing data from your so-called terminal equipment. Unlike a web browser, where cookies can be the primary method for data collection, an app has many more pathways into your personal sphere.

Take an apparently simple weather app as an example. It might request access to your location data (to provide local forecasts), your photos (to let you share weather pictures), your microphone (for voice commands), and your contact list (to share forecasts with friends). Each of these permissions fundamentally involves the app wanting access to information stored on your terminal equipment—your phone.

It does not stop there, though. A modern app can also communicate with multiple different servers simultaneously, use third-party components that collect data in the background, and store information directly on your phone. It can contain hidden tracking mechanisms through various third-party SDKs (Software Development Kits), set its own cookies, and handle sensitive information in ways that are difficult for users to detect.

This is where the role of the ePrivacy Directive becomes so crucial, as it is meant to protect such information from unauthorized access, whether we are talking about a communication app like WhatsApp or an apparently simple weather app.

In December 2020, a significant update around the ePrivacy Directive occurred. The EU implemented the European Electronic Communications Code (EECC)[41]. This made it clear that OTT services like WhatsApp, Skype, and similar communication services, should be subject to the same basic confidentiality requirements as traditional telecom operators.

"But despite this, we see major differences in how various countries have implemented this in practice", says Pols.

What Pols is referring to is perhaps particularly evident in Sweden. When Sweden chose to update its Electronic Communications Act (LEK) in 2022, it opted not to clarify the rules related to OTT services, citing a desire to await the forthcoming ePrivacy Regulation.

"This creates a strange situation where protection for your communication looks different depending on what type of service you use", Pols says and points out how a regular text message via your telecom operator has, in practice, stronger protection than a message via WhatsApp or Messenger— despite the fact that they should be equally protected under the law.

---

[41] A code is a collection of rules and guidelines in a specific area. The EECC is a binding EU directive for the telecommunications sector that complements, but does not replace, the ePrivacy Directive. It consolidates and modernizes previous telecom rules and makes it clear that internet-based communication services are also covered by these regulations.

Metadata or data about data

When Wiesler wiretapped the playwright couple's phone conversations, he gained access not only to the content of their discussions but also to information about who called whom, when the calls occurred, and how long they lasted. In today's digital world, this type of surrounding information is called metadata—data about data.

When I ask whether it matters that oversight or requirements for OTT services lag behind, given that services like WhatsApp use end-to-end encryption, Pols highlights precisely this aspect:

"The fact that the ePrivacy Directive protects your communication over traditional telecom networks means that both the content and metadata are shielded from surveillance. OTT services are also covered by the directive, but to what extent is unclear."

Metadata might seem harmless compared to the actual content of communication, but as the Stasi surveillance demonstrated, patterns in whom someone communicates with, when, and how often can reveal enormous amounts about a person's life and relationships. In today's digital landscape, metadata is even more revealing because it can be collected in a massive scale and analyzed with far more powerful tools.

"The problem is that it is up to each OTT service to specify how they use this data," Pols continues.

"Microsoft wants the metadata from Teams communications. Meta similarly wants access to it from WhatsApp. It is a resource they profit from harvesting", she explains.

Unlike the Stasi, which needed dedicated agents to analyze the information they collected, today's tech companies can automatically analyze metadata from millions of users simultaneously. When a company like Meta can combine WhatsApp metadata with data from Facebook and Instagram, it creates a surveillance capacity that Wiesler's superiors could only have dreamed of.

Nobody wants to give up the metadata

"Even though the OTT discussion is no longer as intense today as it was before the GDPR, the problem persists. A player or service like WhatsApp does not have a clear obligation to respect the confidentiality requirements in the directive. They are not legally required to have end-to-end encryption either", Pols says and continues.

"Unless a member state has chosen to legislate on this and thereby update how the directive is implemented at the national level."

The hope was that the ePrivacy Regulation would resolve this dilemma. But as mentioned, this has not happened. At first because it got stuck in the legislation process in Brussels—specifically in the trilogue, which is a kind of protracted negotiation between the Parliament, Commission, and Council. Since trilogue discussions are conducted behind closed doors, no one knows for certain why they have had such difficulty reaching agreement. But Pols believes the metadata question has likely played and continues to play a crucial role.

"Service providers do not want to lose the metadata and other data. It is a resource they profit from harvesting, and they probably also want to use it in machine learning contexts today."

What Pols describes reveals powerful economic interests working to obstruct the regulation. And it is no secret that lobbying against the directive has been intense and aggressive.

According to *Corporate Europe Observatory*, a staggering 99 percent of all lobbying around ePrivacy came from the industry itself.[42] The publication *Politico* has revealed through leaked documents how Google and Amazon successfully

---

[42] Corporate Europe Observatory. Corporate Europe Observatory: ePrivacy Regulation victim of a "lobby onslaught", European Digital Rights (EDRi) website. Published 2019. https://edri.org/our-work/coe-eprivacy-regulation-victim-of-a-lobby-onslaught/

worked to delay and weaken the regulation from its onset.[43] Additionally, the leading European digital rights organization European Digital Rights (EDRi) has documented how companies systematically influenced both EU institutions and member states. Former GDPR rapporteur Jan Philipp Albrecht, for instance, described the lobbying as "unprecedented" in scope.[44]

It appears to have been a successful lobbying campaign, because in February 2025 the EU Commission pulled the plug on the ePrivacy Regulation. The Commission stated they did this in part because seven years is a long time for lawmakers not to come to an agreement, and in part because they thought that the proposal had become somewhat outdated due to new legislations like the Digital Markets Act and Digital Services Act, which have stepped in and covered some of its scope. Still, this does not mean the final word has been spoken. Among Brussels lawmakers work toward a safer web could intensify during the current mandate period, not least given the backdrop of the November 2024 U.S. election results. And in the meantime, we still have a directive, which is considerably stronger than many realize.

Protecting terminal equipment
— A central component of the directive

To reiterate, the ePrivacy Directive should not be called a "cookie law" simply because it is not just about cookies—it is about surveillance of communication and data collection. Just as Wiesler's surveillance equipment in The Lives of Others could be used to violate people's privacy, today's digital tools

---

[43] Facebook Files and ePrivacy Lobbying – Exposing the power of Big Tech, *Social Europe*. November 2021. https://www.socialeurope.eu/facebook-files-and-eprivacy-lobbying-expose-the-power-of-big-tech

[44] International Association of Privacy Professionals (IAPP). Inside the ePrivacy Regulation's furious lobbying war, IAPP News. Published 2017. https://iapp.org/news/a/inside-the-eprivacy-regulations-furious-lobbying-war

can be used to monitor us. But unlike the GDR era, we now voluntarily carry terminal equipment—our smartphones, smartwatches, connected cars, and more—that can be surveilled through everything from cookies and fingerprinting to SDKs and beyond.

This is where Article 5(3) of the directive comes into play. It concerns the protection of our terminal equipments. As discussed, in our connected world, this includes everything from our smartphones and computers to smart TVs, VR headsets, and IOT-devices. All of these devices are potential windows into our private lives. But technological development never stands still, and new challenges constantly emerge as regulations try to keep pace with technical innovations.

"We have been talking about cookies for so long now that confusion arises when the discussion shifts to other types of tracking mechanisms", says Pols, pointing to the development of server-side tracking.

"For every legal and technical regulation or limitation, a new workaround emerges that tries to circumvent the restrictions. It is like a game of whack-a-mole. When you shut down one way to track users, another pops up somewhere else", she says.

But according to the latest guidelines from the European Data Protection Board (EDPB)[45], the rules are clear—as soon as a device actively takes steps to access information on your terminal equipment, it falls under Article 5(3). It does not matter whether this happens via cookies or by instructing the device to send information to a server—the principle remains the same. User consent is required when someone wants to access or store information on your device.

Another example is "on-device processing," which Apple has invested heavily in. Here, data are processed locally on your phone instead of being sent to the cloud. This does not change

---

[45] European Data Protection Board, Guidelines 2/2023 on Article 5(3) ePrivacy Directive: https://www.edpb.europa.eu/system/files/2024-10/edpb_guidelines_202302_technical_scope_art_53_eprivacydirective_v2_en_0.pdf

the consent requirement. According to EDPB guidelines, it does not matter whether the information stays on the device or is sent elsewhere. As soon as someone wants to store or access information on your terminal equipment, your consent is required. The directive protects your right to control your personal sphere.

What makes the directive so powerful is that it is not locked to any specific technology. Just like the fundamental human rights the directive is based on, it is about the principle—the right to confidential communication and control over our own devices. Whether information is stored, processed, or transmitted, it is the user's right to self-determination that takes center stage.

Does Sweden's wait-and-see approach then not become particularly questionable in light of this? Why did Sweden not choose to clarify the rules around OTT services when the update made it clear that these services are subject to the same confidentiality requirements as traditional telecommunications? They waited for a regulation that never materialized, instead of seizing the opportunity from the get-go, like Denmark.

In 2022 I interviewed Sally Stenberg, a lawyer at the Swedish Post and Telecom Authority (PTS). She explained that Sweden had been slow to act on the cookie issue due to long-standing uncertainty about the division of responsibilities between PTS and what was then the Data Inspection Board (now IMY). She also confirmed that they wanted to await the forthcoming ePrivacy Regulation of the EU. But when the GDPR was implemented in 2018, PTS abandoned its previous interpretation that users should handle cookies through browser settings, and concluded that responsibility should indeed lie with website owners.

Like water in a sieve
— The web leaks personal data

It took as much as 15 years for PTS to catch up with Denmark, and that is disheartening. At the same time, the Swedish Data Protection Authority is way ahead on issuing fines. But neither country have been able to scale their enforcement efforts. This is particularly troubling since legislation and oversight occur in a context where technological development is accelerating. Today, we are in a kind of zero-sum situation online, where the web continues to leak personal data like water in a sieve. Many cookie banners are a scam, and services that enable people to communicate electronically on the web can map and track people's preferences without their awareness of whether or when this occurs. As marketers and website owners, we're deeply complicit in this and benefit from it (at least in the short term).

Would the situation have been any better if history had played out differently? What if the ePrivacy Regulation had taken precedence while the GDPR got stuck in the legislation process? Pols does not have a straight answer to that question. But she believes it would have been enormously beneficial if the ePrivacy Regulation had taken effect as planned the same year the GDPR came into full force.

"That way, oversight in the field could have been centralized in EU countries where fragmentation currently exists, like in Sweden or Poland."

"It likely would have benefited and strengthened the ability and willingness of the authorities to scale their oversight processes."

"But that is not what happened. Instead, we have a situation where the GDPR oversight in the EU has been weak."

"The question I'm grappling with is whether the EU would have needed to implement the Digital Markets Act (DMA) if GDPR compliance had been what it should have been", says

Pols, describing how the Irish data protection authority has left much to be desired.

What Pols is referring to is the monopolistic position that American big tech companies from Silicon Valley hold on internet based electronic communication. These companies—led by Google and Meta—have chosen to place their European headquarters in Ireland and have used their market dominance to dictate the terms for how our respective terminal equipment is used and how our data is collected. Data Protection Commission (DPC) in Ireland, which has the primary responsibility for overseeing these companies under the GDPR, has faced criticism for being overly passive.

The Digital Markets Act (DMA), as mentioned earlier, is the EU's attempt to take a comprehensive approach on the situation by addressing the issue from an antitrust perspective. By classifying the largest tech companies as gatekeepers and imposing special requirements on them, the EU is trying to achieve what neither the ePrivacy Directive nor the GDPR has managed—to curb the tech oligopolies' infrastructure-setting power over the free European Market. DMA (and its sister regulation, the Digital Services Act) is in many ways a game-changer, since the European Commission directly handles oversight rather than leaving it to individual member states.

One way the DMA overlaps with the ePrivacy Directive is in how it handles consent. Under Article 5(2) of the DMA, gatekeepers are not allowed to combine personal data from their different services unless the user has given clear, specific consent that meets GDPR standards. So even if you agree to data processing on one service, that does not automatically mean the company, for example Meta, can use your data across all their other services. This silo rule is meant to stop big tech from pooling data across platforms without your permission. And it is a reasonable requirement, I would say, because it means the responsibility for not tracking and profiling users without informed consent does not fall on ordinary website owners or small companies only, but also on the giant service providers that have become so difficult to avoid.

This also explains why Google rolled out Consent Mode v2 and pushed CMP (consent management platform) partners to adopt it right when the DMA came into force. They needed a way to ensure that any consent users give for sharing or combining their data is valid under both the ePrivacy rules and the new DMA requirements. So it is fair to state that the consent requirements of the DMA upped the consent-game since it is designed to prevent gatekeepers from sidestepping user choice by bundling consents or making it hard to say no. This way, the DMA adds a new layer of control on top of existing privacy laws, guard railing the way the biggest platforms handle and mix personal data across their ecosystems.

When a few large companies control both the platforms we communicate on and the enormous amounts of data about our communication, surveillance risks become tangible and terrifying. The point of the story about Stasi agent Wiesler is ultimately that we as human beings have—and should have—a fundamental right to communicate freely without someone monitoring us and our communication and collecting data about us without permission. When this freedom is eradicated, our lives become constrained—whether the surveillant is a state, an all-encompassing corporation or the two working in tandem.

"With DMA, lawmakers are at least indirectly addressing the shortcomings in the ePrivacy Directive and the challenges of weak GDPR compliance", says Pols, as she continues:

"Fundamentally, this is about the need to limit what kind of information about us that online services are allowed to harvest for profiling and influence, thus essentially making it a democracy issue."

One could argue that when an OTT service, instead of charging for its service, lets users pay with their metadata, it is turning a human right into a commodity, which, by definition, it cannot be.

When the service then uses these data against the user across other platforms in its ecosystem—for instance, to serve ads for a particular political party or for organizations seeking to suppress voter turnout among individuals who meet specific criteria, the stakes become clear. This is the kind of scenario that the ePrivacy Directive's protection of terminal equipment and confidential communication was designed to prevent—but as we have seen throughout this chapter, it requires both robust implementation and vigilant oversight to work in practice. As do most laws.

III

The Coffee
& The Cakes

7. What is a cookie?

What the hell is a cookie?

On a sweltering summer day at Almedalen, an annual national political festival in Sweden dating back to the 1960's, I found myself on a stage discussing online tracking and privacy. The panel included a representative from the Swedish Data Protection Authority (IMY), a representative from Google, and me. We were there to tackle one of the most complex and challenging issues in today's digital world: How the web leaks personal data like a sieve, and why a business model that respects user privacy is fundamentally a sustainability issue.

I was supposed to illuminate the friction between two critical needs: protecting users' personal data and running profitable digital marketing. But what should have been a discussion about the future of the web and users' rights, ended up (at least toward the end) focusing more on that ever-present, all-too familiar, and sometimes downright annoying cookie banner. That is what the online audience kept asking about.

This threw me off my game, and I left the debate with a queasy feeling in my stomach. What gnawed at me was that I should have known better. This was the most fundamental question—the one I was most grounded in and had the answers to. Yet I'd gotten flustered. Why? Because I'd overcomplicated it.

On one hand, you could argue that few people understand the complexity of this issue and how democratically charged it really is. It is not for nothing that the ePrivacy Regulation, for instance, remained stuck (and died) in the trilogue. On the other hand, the whole thing is not particularly difficult to grasp—you just have to have the guts to point at the elephant in the room while discussing what a better alternative might look like.

Anyway, what makes the cookie—or online tracking— question (seemingly) tricky is that it is nearly impossible to have any opinion about it unless you simultaneously dive into how the internet, or the web actually works. The backstory of this information technology is crucial. It is intertwined with the story of lawmakers' intentions and what various stakeholders in the internet economy want, from users and advertisers to big tech companies and platforms.

So, let us start with the most fundamental question in this story, and then move on to whether the days of cookies are numbered.

What exactly is a cookie?

A cookie usually gets described as a
small information file
script that gets placed on your browser
very small text file
with the addition:
"...that the browser creates when you visit a website."

In my earlier attempts to get a handle on the cookie concept, these kinds of introductions triggered my procrastination nerve. But then one day, the penny finally dropped. It hit me that you cannot understand what a cookie is without understanding what the internet—or rather, the World Wide Web— is. Technically a cookie is secondary; what is interesting is **why** it exists. But before you can talk about the cookie's genesis and reason for being, it helps to grasp the difference between the internet and the www. At least, that is how it was for me.

The short version goes something like this: The internet is the world's digital infrastructure. On this infrastructure, you can run different kinds of vehicles or modes of transportation. The World Wide Web (www) is one of those vehicles on the internet. Email is another vehicle, mobile applications are another, and so on. In other words, the World Wide Web is one of the most popular vehicles—one of the most revolutionary inventions (built on top of) the internet.

The longer account is a journey in time that begins in the 1960s ARPANET and runs through the 1980s TCP protocol and DNS systems, and especially through Tim Berners-Lee's www-http protocol. The latter opened up web browsing in the 1990s, first significantly through the Mosaic browser, and then via Netscape. And it was through the entrepreneurial spirit of Netscape that the HTTP cookie came into the world. This is where the story of web tracking begins. The most fascinating aspect about this story is how idealistic and visionary some of the key players were (and still are).

When Lou Montulli developed the cookie in 1994, he was 23 years old. And web browsing was in desperate need of better "memory." Like other pioneers who paved the way for the web, Montulli was driven to create an open digital infrastructure that would benefit everyone. He was also aware of the privacy risks inherent in an open network. He believed that the web should not be used to track people through their browsers against their will or without their consent. He and the Netscape team therefore rejected simpler solutions because their memory span would have been too powerful. They would have made it possible for outside third parties to track visitors in a limitless way—following them across all the websites they visited. So, with caution and careful consideration, he chose to develop the cookie, or what are now called session cookies, for their web browser and simultaneously released the solution for other browsers to implement. The whole point of the cookie was that it could—and can—exchange information between the visitor's browser and the site they visited, so the site would remember that the surfer had been there before. It is simply practical.

Say, without cookies a shopping cart in an online store cannot remember that you have put items in it if you navigate to another page on the same website or take a detour to other websites. So, cookies came into the world, or rather into web browsers, to radically simplify web browsing. Many of the functions we take for granted today when moving from page to page would not work without Montulli's and Netscape's decision to let their browser handle cookies. A cookie is not some entity flying around on the internet. It is a memory file that gets permission to function through a browser like Google's Chrome or Apple's Safari.

The cookie is hacked

Just two years after the Netscape cookie saw the light of day, a more invasive cookie had been developed. A cookie solution that made it possible to track surfers' activities from one website to all other websites. The third-party cookie had arrived.[46]

It could be traced back to the advertising industry's desire to target specific ads to specific visitors. Thus, an individual who had browsed a page for golf shoes, could receive an ad for golf shoes targeted at them in a feed on a completely different website.

Montulli says they were caught off guard. At Netscape, where they now were under pressure from the competing Microsoft Internet Explorer browser, there were only few people who had time to do anything about the situation. It fell to Montulli to decide how to proceed. As he saw it, he now had three choices:

1. Do nothing; let the advertising industry have their cookie feast.
2. Block third-party cookies on their browser (Netscape)
3. A middle way where Netscape users could control which cookies (from which websites) were allowed to reside on their browser. While also being able to block third-party cookies for certain websites, or for all websites.

They went with option 3.

---

[46] See for example: Hidden Heroes, The Magic Cookie: How Lou Montulli cured the web's amnesia. Published, 2022.
https://hiddenheroes.netguru.com/lou-montulli

Today, with a little effort, you can check how many cookies are stored in your browser (see page 120), and this originates from a standard set by Netscape.

That Montulli and other idealistic internet visionaries cared about user privacy did not mean he was a dogmatic privacy advocate. They were driven to realize the potential that the open web held. And if the World Wide Web was going to succeed as a concept, they reasoned, it needed to benefit those who used it, which meant it needed a sustainable business model.

For many websites, advertising revenue was the only source of income. Advertising was the price you had to pay for the web to provide everyone with an unlimited ocean of information. The third-party cookie could therefore be seen as a harmless enabler, at least if users had the ability to opt out of them. And yet, the third-party cookie is being phased out—sort of. Or maybe not at all, really.

8. The cookie death

The never-ending story.

The days of the third-party cookie have long been numbered. At least it seemed that way until the summer of 2024, when the march toward its demise suddenly lost momentum. But before we examine why this cookie is proving so hard to kill (spoiler alert: it is about money), let us first understand why the question of its death became an issue at all.

The answer can be linked to two factors: growing public unease and intensified pressure from regulators and lawmakers.

People's discomfort is easy to understand. Internet tracking has become pervasive and intrusive, enabling behavioral advertising companies to build comprehensive profiles of individuals—capturing even the smallest details of their online lives. The situation has worsened since the controversial Target incident, in which the retailer mailed baby product ads to a teenage girl, to the dismay of her parents. The programmatic advertising industry, which can create detailed profiles through cookies based on even highly sensitive personal data, freely shares this information with companies worldwide including those in countries like Russia and China, where the state has legal authority to access that data. This makes the cookie question both a national security issue and a cybersecurity risk.

Meanwhile, regulatory authorities are in some ways catching up. They are not just issuing guidelines about the interplay between the GDPR and the ePrivacy Directive—which requires website owners to obtain valid consent before placing cookies—they are also handing out substantial fines to those who break the rules. And, as mentioned, new regulations like the Digital Markets Act and Digital Services Act have also begun to put pressure on the major tech platforms, particularly from an antitrust perspective. So, there is increased pressure for an adtech monopolist like Google to at least appear like they were trying to do something about the issue.

GDPR was adopted by the European Parliament in 2016 and went into full effect in 2018. The "cookie death" issue began in 2017 when Apple decided to block third-party cookies in Safari. Two years later, Firefox chose to do the same. (Incidentally, Firefox was developed from Netscape's open-source code.) But it was not until Google announced they wanted to phase out third-party cookies, first proclaimed in 2020, that the market began talking about a so-called "cookie death" in more fateful terms. There were two reasons for this. A) Chrome dominated (still dominates) the global browser market with roughly a 63 percent market share. B) The industry could not quite figure out how to continue with targeted advertising on the "open web" without the third-party cookie system.

On the other hand, the third-party cookie has been under scrutiny since it first saw the light of day during the Netscape era. Today's discourse is rooted in the same dilemma that Montulli faced and articulated at the very dawn of the web. It is still true that if third-party cookies are phased out, other tracking technologies exist. In other words, solutions can be considered more invasive and questionable from a privacy perspective, and not as easy for individual visitors to block.

Also note that there is no legal obligation to eliminate third-party cookies. The cookie as such is not "illegal." What is not permitted is placing cookies on peoples' devices, collecting personal data, tracking people, and building profiles of individuals—without their consent. The underlying issue concerns a fundamental conflict in the web's ecosystem: How do we create an open and accessible web that simultaneously respects users' privacy?

We have grown accustomed to a web that is financed through tracking-based advertising. But this business model conflicts with every person's right to privacy and data security. The challenge lies in finding an economic model that can finance a free and open internet without compromising users' right to privacy and confidentiality. Is it possible to strike a balance between commercial interests and personal privacy?

Can the web continue to be reasonably "free" and open to everyone without extensive data collection? Should it be?

Montulli said early on that there is no technical solution to the tracking problem. Instead, he emphasized that lawmakers must take responsibility by keeping pace with technological development and enacting reasonable privacy laws, and for the public to keep pressure on lawmakers and companies.[47]

What is illegal offline, must be illegal online. American lawmakers at the federal level still have not heeded his call. In Europe, as we have seen, they were more tuned in.

Cookies with coffee

The "cookie death" is a confusing concept because it gives the impression that cookies as such are disappearing—all kinds of cookies. As you have noted, there are different types of cookies. And what browsers like Safari and Firefox have primarily restricted is the third-party cookie.

This means first-party cookies are still embraced by every browser on the market. Does that mean the third-party cookie phase-out is (or was) not such a big deal after all?

Both yes and no.

Remember how I wrote that the technical explanation of a cookie felt too abstract for me, and it was not until I understood why the cookie came to be that the penny dropped? Now that we understand the original session, the purpose of the cookie was to give web browsing experience a better memory, and that it was later "hacked" so we got a third-party cookie that enabled targeted advertising, we need to return to the technical distinction to bring it home, because it is not entirely obvious how a third-party cookie differs from a first-party cookie. And the devil is in the details.

---

[47] See Lou Montulli's own blog: The irregular musings of Lou Montulli, The reasoning behind web cookies. Published, May 14, 2013.
https://montulli.blogspot.com/2013/05/the-reasoning-behind-web-cookies.html

To understand the difference, we need coffee with our cookies, but only when JavaScript is involved. First-party cookies can be placed in your browser either by JavaScript code embedded on the website you are visiting, or directly by the website's server through HTTP headers, which does not require any JavaScript at all.

Java(script)[48] is also, as you know, another word for coffee. Is that why the files are called cookies? No, Montulli chose to call his invention cookie as a reference to earlier days of computing, when machines passed bits of code back and forth for the purpose of identification. Because earlier programmers called the exchanged data "magic cookies".[49] Nevertheless, cookies very often come with coffee. When as a website owner you integrate services like Google Analytics, Hotjar, or Facebook on your website, it happens through JavaScript in the page's HTML code. This script enables the service to place cookies in the visitor's browser, regardless of which browser is being used.

How many cookies a particular service provider places, what purposes they serve, and how long they stay active depends on who the service provider is. Cookies placed by HubSpot do their "thing" while cookies placed by Meta/Facebook do theirs.

Also note that these cookies are usually defined as first-party cookies, since they are deployed by your domain, i.e., the website the visitor directly interacts with, thanks to the script you have chosen to activate (by placing it on your site). This makes you, the website owner, and your domain "the first party".

Third-party cookies, on the other hand, often gain access to your visitors' browsers via external services embedded on your website, such as:

---

[48] That is, JavaScript. JavaScript and Java are two different programming languages despite the similarity in names.

[49] *New York Times,* Giving web a memory costs its users privacy. Published September 2001. https://www.nytimes.com/2001/09/04/business/giving-web-a-memory-cost-its-users-privacy.html

- o A YouTube video
- o A social media widget
- o Google Maps
- o An advertising widget from an ad network

These external services[50] place cookies in your visitors' browsers for their own purposes, making it possible for the providers to follow an individual from website to website to target various kinds of ads, for example.

But at the same time, the difference between a first-party cookie and a third-party cookie is not always this "simple".

Even though the discrepancy between first-party and third-party cookies primarily concerns in which domain technically and legally the cookie is placed and for what purpose, the scripts you intentionally place through your website can also set third-party cookies. In other words, they are placed by a domain other than yours with the ability to do the type of cross-site tracking that has made them passé in certain browsers.

Are you with me?

So, a service can place multiple cookies through its script, and some of them can be categorized as third-party cookies. And to complicate things further, a script from a third-party domain can also place cookies that are defined as strictly necessary, or just functional cookies.

As a website owner, you therefore need to stay on your toes when calibrating the services you use so you understand what they do and why. This becomes easier to manage if you use a legitimate consent platform—a so-called CMP (Consent Management Platform). That is a platform that provides your website with a proper "cookie banner". The serious players in this market scan your entire domain and classify and categorize

---

[50] Even seemingly innocent resources like external fonts, CDNs (Content Delivery Network), or embedded widgets can involve the transmission of user data and may use JavaScript or server requests that result in cookies or other tracking mechanisms being set.

all scripts, while simultaneously creating a dynamic cookie policy that categorizes all scripts and their respective cookies according to what type of cookie it is and what the service aims to do. It is also a good way to get an overview of what kind of products and services you have running on your website. A company, which has hired several different web agencies over the years might have countless scripts just laying around collecting digital dust.

Also note that cookies are classified in more ways than just which domain places them—for example, based on their lifespan and purpose. This is not just a technical detail; these categories are required by law (ePrivacy, GDPR, DMA) so that users can understand and control what is happening with their data. In the final section of the book, *The Privacy Balance*, I will walk you through how to get control over the services you use and the cookies they place.

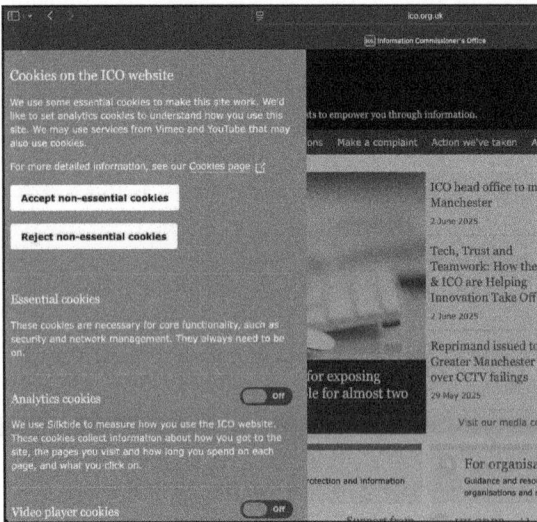

Here is an example of a cookie banner. This one appears on the website of the Information Commissioner's Office, which is the UK Data Protection Authority.

Worth noting: Before privacy laws and browser restrictions started tightening the rules, it was common to find cookies set to last for decades—sometimes with expiration dates 20, 50, or even 99 years into the future. Today, browsers like Chrome and Safari limit cookie lifespans to a maximum of 400 days or even just seven days in some cases.

What would have replaced the third-party cookie in Chrome?

When Firefox chose to block third-party cookies by default in 2019, they did so by implementing their Enhanced Tracking Protection (ETP) feature. This is a protocol that encompasses far more than merely the status of third-party cookies. Same story with Apple's Safari, which with its Intelligent Tracking Prevention (ITP) in 2020 did much more than "simply" block third-party cookies.

Neither ITP nor ETP kills the possibility for targeted advertising outright in their respective browsers. But they make it challenging to show targeted ads to individuals based on their browsing history. Other smaller browsers have taken similar measures.

With Chrome, however, we have a completely different situation.

Google did not want to throw the baby out with the bathwater, eliminating third-party cookies without finding a system that could replace the value they create for advertisers, and thus for Google itself. So, they reinvented the wheel and called it Privacy Sandbox.

Google is the world's largest ad-tech player and can therefore be said to have a genuine interest in finding a new web standard that does not "kill" this revenue stream. At the same time, as the UK Competition and Markets Authority (CMA) investigation shows, a giant like Google does not have nearly as much to lose as the independent ad-tech companies operating "outside" Google's ecosystem. Since Chrome is massive, and Google as an ad-tech company is practically a monopoly, they cannot just roll out Privacy Sandbox willy-nilly, because it would affect every player and company on the ad-tech market.

The art of having your cake and eating it too

What exactly is Privacy Sandbox? And how is, or rather was, it supposed to replace the third-party cookie?

For several years, Google has been trying to find a way to have the cookie and eat it too, so to speak, through an industry-wide collaboration called Privacy Sandbox (PS).

Privacy Sandbox has been an iterative process where various APIs have been developed and distributed for testing. This process appeared to reach a milestone in mid-2023 when the initiative announced the release of six new cookie-replacing APIs for Chrome version 115:

1. Topics API
2. Protected audience
3. Attribution reporting
4. Private aggregation
5. Shared storage
6. Fenced frames

There are more APIs in the workings. However, the initiative has experienced ongoing delays and was postponed indefinitely on the summer of 2024. And in April 2025 Google threw in the towel and said that they were not going to deprecate the third-party cookie after all. The Privacy Sandbox project is still running though, now under the broader and more vague aim to make Chrome more privacy-friendly—while enabling target advertising that is less invasive.

However, even though the third-party cookie in Chrome is not going away, the details of how it was intended to "go away" is quite interesting. Details matter greatly. A closer examination of each Privacy Sandbox API reveals how the web's advertising ecosystem functions today—and what it takes, or would have taken, to keep this market dynamic rolling in a way that benefits, at least, Google.

Topics API

The Topics API is like a digital library where your interests are sorted into broad shelf categories—such as "Food & Drink," "Transportation," or "Fitness"—based on your recent browsing activity. For example:

- o If you frequently visit cooking sites, you might be placed in the "Food & Drink" category
- o If you follow fitness blogs, you would be grouped under "Fitness."

What makes Topics unique is that your browser (Chrome) keeps track of these interest categories locally, acting like a personal librarian who knows your reading habits but never shares the full list with anyone else. When you visit a participating website, the browser shares only a small, rotating set of your current topics—never your full browsing history or sensitive details—helping advertisers to show relevant ads while protecting your privacy.

Protected audience API

If the Topics API is like a library of broad interests, the Protected Audience API is more like joining specialized clubs—created by advertisers—based on your actions on specific sites.

For example, if you browse running shoes on a retailer's website, that site can ask your browser: "Can we add this user to the 'Running Enthusiasts' club?" Your browser then stores this membership locally, without sharing your identity or browsing history with the retailer or any adtech company.

When you visit other sites, your browser can run a private, on-device auction among ads targeted to your "clubs" (interest groups) to decide which ad to show you—such as a reminder for the running shoes you browsed. The entire process happens inside your browser, so your membership and activity are, allegedly, not shared with third parties.

Unlike traditional remarketing, where your data is sent to adtech platforms via third-party cookies, the Protected Audience API is claimed to keep your group memberships private and on-device. Advertisers never see who is in each group; they only know their ad is being shown to someone in the group they defined.

The big difference from before is that Chrome "owns" the information about the visitor's interests—not the advertisers or adtech platforms. But since Google is the world's largest ad-tech player, there is a conflict of interest here, to put it mildly.

Attribution reporting API

While the two first APIs are about categorizing or profiling without profiling what visitors are interested in, this API is about helping advertisers and publishers to understand which ads work best—without revealing who looked at the ad and who converted.

Private aggregation API

This one is claimed to work like the Attribution Reporting API but in an aggregated way—where the reporting is based on data from the Topics API and Shared Storage (see below). So, instead of reporting on single user actions, this API collects and summarizes data from sources like Shared Storage or other Privacy Sandbox APIs. It then adds privacy-preserving "noise" to ensure that only broad trends and totals are reported, and not information about specific users.

Shared storage API

The Shared Storage API can be compared to a safety deposit box for web information. Just as a safety deposit box can contain valuables without the bank knowing exactly what is inside, this API allows websites to store information about visitors' activities in what Google claims is a secure way. For example:

o   You browse winter sports gear on an online store
o   The store saves information about your interest in winter sports gear in Shared Storage
o   Later, when you visit a different website that displays ads, the ad system can use Shared Storage to determine which products to show you—without directly accessing your personal data
o   The advertiser receives only aggregated or limited information, so your privacy is supposedly protected even as relevant ads are displayed

The idea is that Shared Storage should give advertisers the ability to work with cross-site advertising and analytics while, Google protects the visitor's privacy.

Fenced frames API

This API is pretty easy to understand of the bat. With the Fenced Frames API, websites can display ads without the ad window being able to track or collect information about the visitor viewing the ad or track the visitor across the entire web. Think of it as "a privacy-secure iframe."[51]

What "cookie death" would have meant for you—would have depended on who "you" are

Google has played the lead role in the story about the third-party cookie-phase-out. This is inevitable since Google is justifiably described as an oligopoly when it is not being described as a monopoly. This is true, not only because of how the antitrust work in the UK has led Google to indefinitely delay the Privacy Sandbox initiative, but perhaps mostly because of two massive antitrust lawsuits against Google in the United States.

The Search Monopoly Case: In August 2024, a federal judge ruled that Google has illegally monopolized the search market. The U.S. Department of Justice (DOJ) responded by demanding that Google's parent company, Alphabet, sell off Chrome entirely. They have also proposed splitting Android from Google's other products. Google, unsurprisingly, has pushed back with a counterproposal: Instead of breaking up, they would modify their exclusive licensing deals with companies like Apple and Mozilla, and additionally change their contracts with Android phone manufacturers.[52] As of this writing (June 2025), no final breakup order has been issued.

---

[51] An iframe, or Inline Frame, is an HTML element used to embed things like YouTube or Vimeo clips, or ads, etc., on your website. It isIt is a handy way to seamlessly integrate external content. The problem is that iframes are not very secure from a privacy perspective and can also create several security vulnerabilities. They can be used to execute malicious scripts and steal visitors' user data, for example.

[52] Yes, Google pays enormous sums to keep Google Search as the default in Safari and Firefox (Mozilla's browser). Apple alone pockets around $20 billion per year for this arrangement.

The Adtech Monopoly Case: The second lawsuit, launched in September 2024, targets Google's stranglehold on digital advertising. Here, the DOJ argues that Google controls every link in the advertising chain—from the tools publishers use to sell ad space, to the platforms advertisers use to buy it, to the marketplace where they meet. In April 2025, another federal judge agreed: Google holds a monopoly in adtech too.

Google is appealing both rulings

Even though these are two separate cases, they are deeply interconnected—Google's search engine is obviously a core part of their ad-tech empire. But the second case is particularly revealing because it exposes how Google strategically built a position where they control every single link in the digital advertising chain—the very ecosystem of which third-party cookies have been, and still are, a cornerstone. Google owns the tools that publishers use to sell ad space, the tools that advertisers use to buy ads, AND the entire marketplace where buyers and sellers meet. That means control over a market worth over $700 billion.

Hence the cookie death story ties into the warped dynamics of the digital ad-tech market. The burial of the third-party cookie in Chrome would have been a complex, multi-faceted process which would have affected each stakeholder on the advertising market differently. With stakeholders I mean the consumer, the marketer, the ad-tech provider and the publisher.

The consumer and the third-party cookie

During the first quarter of 2024, Google began testing Privacy Sandbox on one percent of Chrome users. These users encountered questions about their preferences and consent through a feature called "tracking protection."

The feature communicated with users directly from the address bar of the browser, informed them that they were now "browsing with enhanced privacy." Users could then either accept these new settings or adjust them according to their preferences.

This was Google's attempt to ease users into a post-cookie world; however, it never reached full deployment. When Google announced in July 2024 that they were shelving the third-party cookie phase-out indefinitely, these early tests became a fascinating glimpse into what might have been. And then the company pivoted to a different approach: Instead of eliminating third-party cookies entirely, they said they would give users more granular control over their tracking preferences, a change that could still reshape how online advertising works.

But even this scaled-back vision raises questions. If Google had followed through with full Privacy Sandbox deployment, what would it have meant for the average Chrome user? The early tests suggested a world where your browser would become more protective by default, but where the underlying advertising infrastructure—dominated by Google itself—would remain largely intact. Users would have gained some privacy theater while Google maintained its stranglehold on digital advertising through new, proprietary channels.

For consumers, the real question was never whether Privacy Sandbox would work technically—it was whether it would meaningfully shift power away from surveillance capitalism or simply give it a fresh coat of paint. After all, at the end of the day, Google's effort with Privacy Sandbox did not change the core logic of its business model, where the user is the product.

The marketer and the third-party cookie

One hundred percent of users were supposed to experience the "cookie-free" existence in Chrome by December 2024. But that did not happen. Had Google followed through with their plan to phase out third-party cookies and replace them with Privacy Sandbox APIs, you as a marketer would have primarily needed to understand how the Google products you use—or want to continue using—function in this new landscape. For instance, how would Google's web analytics tools fit into Chrome's new ecosystem? If you were running GA4, you would have needed to pay special attention to Consent Mode v2—and frankly, you still do.[53] This remains a smart starting point since Consent Mode v2 is something Google has chosen to go all-in on, with or without the Privacy Sandbox.[54] As previously mentioned, the reason is that Google (as a gatekeeper), with the DMA now in force, must be able to prove that users have given valid consent for data collection and use across its services. This is why marketers not having implemented Consent Mode v2, were told that they would lose access to key analytics and advertising features, as Google would restrict data collection for EU users unless the right consent signals were in place.

At the same time, it would have been wise to familiarize oneself with the concept of first-party data and how to create a sustainable first-party data strategy. And despite Google walking back the third-party cookie deprecation, this is still reasonable advice. After all, Chrome is not the only browser on the market. The reality is that even without full deployment of the Privacy Sandbox, the writing is on the wall. Safari and Firefox have already eliminated third-party cookies. Other browsers are following suit. And Google's own pivot does not eliminate the fundamental market pressures pushing toward a post-cookie advertising landscape.

For marketers, this means the core challenge remains unchanged: How do you build effective, privacy-respecting marketing strategies that do not depend on invasive tracking?

---

[53] Consent Mode v2 is an API, which Google requires all GA4 and Google Ads users to integrate into their Consent Management Platform. Failure to comply typically results in reduced data visibility and campaign effectiveness—Google's way of ensuring adoption without calling it a penalty.
[54] Since you are likely dependent on Google Ads for your advertising, you will need to grapple with Consent Mode v2—especially if you want to maintain visibility into your web analytics and ad performance. This becomes even more critical as browsers continue restricting third-party tracking, regardless of whether Google's Privacy Sandbox ever sees the light of day.

Whether that future arrives through Google's APIs, browser restrictions in general, or regulatory pressure, the destination is the same.

The adtech companies and the third-party cookie

At the heart of the cookie question lies advertising. Adtech providers has relied on third-party cookies to offer behavioral advertising solutions (to both publishers and advertisers), based on information about where a visitor is located, which pages they visit, what products they buy, which device they are browsing on, and so forth.

Third-party cookies enable the automatic buying and placement of ads in real-time, or they collect the data needed for advertisers to bid on ad placements the moment a webpage loads.

Third-party cookies are thus crucial to multiple aspects of digital advertising. They are used to identify visitors, limit how often a user sees an ad (frequency capping), measure how well ads perform, and track which ads lead to purchases. They also make it possible to target ads to the right audiences and synchronize data between different advertising systems, such as demand-side platforms (DSPs) and supply-side platforms (SSPs).[55]

But note that it is the adtech providers operating outside the walled gardens who are most acutely and directly affected by any potential elimination of third-party cookies and other

---

[55] DSP, i.e., Demand-Side Platform, is a platform used by advertisers to automatically purchase ad space from multiple publishers simultaneously. SSP, i.e., Supply-Side Platform, is a platform used by publishers—those who sell ad space—to automatically auction off their digital ad inventory to maximize revenue for each ad placement. DSPs represent the demand side, where advertisers seek to buy ad impressions at the best price. SSPs represent the supply side, where publishers strive to sell ad impressions at the highest price.

browser-based tracking restrictions. This is because walled gardens—like Google's Play Store, Google's own adtech ecosystem, Google's YouTube, Meta's Facebook, Apple's App Store, and other such closed platforms or ecosystems—have direct access to enormous amounts of first-party data, which they can capitalize on in an era without third-party cookies.

Adtech companies started to adapt to the anticipated shift in various ways. Some begun focusing on first-party data— information that websites themselves collect about their visitors—and offer tools and services that help other companies manage this type of data. Some also began using so-called Data Clean Rooms, where companies can supposedly share and analyze data together in a secure way that protects user privacy.

Others have developed new ways to identify users as a replacement for third-party cookies. Examples include solutions like Unified ID and ID5. The hope is that these new identities will become a new non-cookie standard that better respects people's right to personal privacy. However, these new ID solutions face their own challenges, since it is fundamentally very difficult to—well, you know—keep your cake and eat it too.

The publisher and the third-party cookie

The web lowered barriers to entry for anyone wanting to create and distribute content. It became a network built on convenience and immediacy. And it has been revolutionary.

For traditional journalistic publishers and media houses, this development has meant declining advertising revenues. They have been forced to adapt their business models, not just by going online, but by trying to survive in what can best be described today as a codependent relationship with the so-called walled gardens.[56]

---

[56] A walled garden is a digital platform or ecosystem tightly controlled by a specific provider, which restricts users' access to external content, services, and data. Within this closed environment, all user interactions—including

The challenge for legacy news media was not the emergence of the web itself, but rather the advertising model that made big tech companies big: tracking and collecting personal data *en masse*. Third-party cookies made the web lucrative for adtech companies, both inside and outside walled gardens, who could offer hyper-personalized advertising based on detailed user profiling.

Whether third-party cookies would eventually be phased out or not—or whether Google is ordered to sell parts of its business—the rigid threat to quality journalism and traditional media remains. Google's and Meta's surveillance economy continues to challenge media houses regardless.

Whether the third-party cookie would ever be phased out or not, the dilemma remains the same.

The problem is that established publishers are woven into the adtech systems that Google dominates, making them just as driven to get readers to click "accept all" cookies on news sites as Google and other adtech companies are. If publishers want to become more profitable and freer, they need to think bigger and more outside the box than they have so far. While following the legal challenges pressuring both Google and Meta today, they need to consider how they might reinvent themselves if anything were possible.

So, what happens now?

First, publishers have spent the past two decades adapting and diversifying their revenue streams by exploring paywalls, sponsored (native) content, and other approaches to create

---

content consumption and advertising—are managed using the proprietary tools and systems of the platform. The provider controls what users see, how data is collected and used, and what advertisers can access. Major examples include Google, Facebook (Meta), Amazon, and Apple, which operate vast walled gardens to maximize user engagement and advertising revenue. Advertisers and publishers must use these built-in technologies of the platform and can only access aggregated, non-identifiable data for campaign insights—never raw user-level data. This closed approach enables the companies to leverage their extensive first-party data for highly targeted advertising, while limiting interoperability and competition from external services.

added value for their readers and advertisers. In doing so, they have learned the value of first-party data—firsthand information about their customers and audiences. And first-party data with explicit consent.

But then what?

Since we now face new challenges and opportunities from generative AI, layered on top of the online tracking discourse and monopoly questions, no one has all the answers. It may sound cliché, but in many ways, publishers need to ask themselves what they truly want, how they envision quality journalism thriving in the future, and what this requires— politically, legally, and technically.[57]

Why did the CMA stop Google?

As mentioned, Privacy Sandbox can be described as Google's attempt to want to keep the cake and eat it too: offering an alternative to third-party cookies that (perhaps) respects user privacy while enabling the type of targeted advertising the web has grown accustomed to. In February 2024, the UK's Competition and Markets Authority (CMA) stepped in to make sure Privacy Sandbox wouldn't tilt the ad market even further in Google's favour. The regulator told Google it had to design and roll out the system in a way that did not give its own advertising products, like Google Ad Manager, an edge over everyone else. Google said it still planned to phase out third-party cookies in the second half of 2024 but admitted this depended on meeting the CMA's requirements and addressing its concerns.[58]

---

[57] See also Chapter 16, where lawyer and adtech expert Arielle Garcia deepens the discussion around publishers' future role in the digital media landscape.
[58] UK Competition and Markets Authority, Google's Privacy Sandbox Commitments (February 4, 2024): Google agreed not to develop Privacy Sandbox in a way that strengthens its advertising dominance, including through Google Ad Manager. See Appendix 1A:
https://assets.publishing.service.gov.uk/media/62052c6a8fa8f510a204374a/10 0222_Appendix_1A_Google_s_final_commitments.pdf

The CMA, however, was not convinced. In their comprehensive 99-page report, the authority scrutinized the entire arsenal of APIs that Privacy Sandbox comprises. Their conclusion was that these tools, Google's assurances notwithstanding, risked further strengthening of the company's dominant position in digital advertising.

In July 2024, Google acknowledged they had been forced to reconsider. And as you already know, instead of a total phase-out of third-party cookies, they presented a new strategy where Chrome users would have greater ability to make their own choices about web browsing.

I find it telling that it was ultimately a competition authority that slammed the brakes on how Google wanted to phase out the third-party cookie in Chrome. While the cookie question is often viewed through a privacy lens, it fundamentally also concerns whether Google's business model is sustainable for the web as a marketplace. As we have established, Google already controls the digital advertising chain. The CMA's decision demonstrates that the question of the future of the third-party cookies cannot be separated from the larger question of how we want power over the internet to be distributed.

For those of us who have slogged through the CMA's report and delved into the Privacy Sandbox initiative, it is hard not to marvel at how technically convoluted it is to want to keep your cake and eat it too. It brings us back to Montulli, who early on emphasized that there are no technical solutions to this challenge. Instead, it is about political and economic trade-offs where different societal interests must be balanced against each other.

9. Is the pixel tastier than the cookie?

No, it is not.

"You bought a chlamydia test, the pharmacy told Facebook."

That was one of the headlines when Swedish Radio revealed in 2022 how Swedish pharmacies were sharing sensitive personal data with the social media giant. This was not some minor incident—the investigation showed that information of up to 900,000 customers had been transferred to Facebook over a two-year period. Everything from shopping cart contents and social security numbers to information about sensitive products like self-tests for sexually transmitted diseases was sent to Facebook, linked to unique ID numbers for each visitor.

When Swedish Radio started asking questions, the pharmacy quickly shut off the tracking tool. Several pharmacies reported the data breach to the Swedish Data Protection Authority (IMY), which later resulted in million-kronor fines—37 million SEK for state-owned Apoteket AB and 8 million for online pharmacy Apohem.

But how could this happen? Let us untangle that by clarifying what a pixel actually is.

From pixel to script

Once upon a time, there was a technology called a pixel or web beacon,[59] for example, used to measure traffic on a website. The name came from placing a tiny image element—1x1 pixel—on the website, invisible to the naked eye. This simple method was primarily used to track whether someone had visited a webpage

---

[59] The pixel goes by many names. Besides web beacon, it was also known as a web bug, pixel tag, or clear GIF. The name "web beacon" refers to it acting like a lighthouse or signal on the web that could track user activity without being visible to the user.

or opened an email. The pixel has existed since the early 1990s, just like the cookie in its basic form. However, the so-called "Facebook Pixel" is not a pixel in the original sense at all. Instead, it is a piece of JavaScript code that you add to your website—just like the script provided by for example Google Analytics. This script does much more than the original 1x1 image ever could. It can track a wide range of user actions, trigger different events, and set cookies for more advanced tracking and ad optimization. In other words, the Facebook Pixel has kept the name from the early tracking pixel, which can feel misleading.

However, in some discourses the term pixel is used as an umbrella term for different tracking technologies.

Is the Facebook pixel more Invasive than other scripts?

When it comes to data collection and online tracking, the Facebook pixel stands out in several ways. It is not because it is technically more advanced than other scripts, but rather because of how it is designed and the context in which it operates. Here are three decisive factors that make the Facebook pixel particularly problematic:

1. All responsibility falls on the website owner
Facebook has chosen a strategy where the entire burden of configuring the script falls on the website owner. This might seem reasonable at first glance—after all, it is the website owner who controls their own site. But in practice, this creates several problems.

To start with, the script comes with extensive default features that must be actively turned off if you want to limit data collection. The documentation is also technically complex and requires deep understanding of both GDPR and tracking technology. Even small configuration mistakes can lead to extensive data collection, and since Facebook continuously updates the functionality of the script, consistent monitoring from the website owner is required.

This stands in contrast to other analytics scripts that often have more limited default settings, which can then be expanded as desired.

2. Matching capabilities on steroids

Facebook's ability to connect and analyze data is exceptional, largely thanks to the company's enormous user base and broad presence across the web. When a website activates the Facebook pixel, it opens the door to extensive profiling. As the company's founder and majority owner, Mark Zuckerberg, wrote in an internal message during the early days of Facebook, when he was a student at Harvard:

"They 'trust me'. Dumb fucks."[60]

Facebook can link a user's activity on an e-commerce site with that person's Facebook profile, Instagram account, and WhatsApp activity (you know, the metadata we discussed in Chapter 8). The script registers detailed information about which products a person looks at, how long they linger on different pages, what they put in their shopping cart, and which purchases they complete, for example. For logged-in Facebook users, this activity can also be tracked across multiple devices— cell phone, work computer, personal laptop, and tablet.

Let us look at a concrete example: If you visit an online store for children's clothes, the Facebook pixel can register that you are looking at clothes in size 86, spending extra time on the page with winter jackets, and finally buying overalls. This

---

[60] Kara Swisher, Burn Book, 2024. The quote stems from an IM conversation Zuckerberg had during the early days of Facebook, when he was a student at Harvard. The conversation was about how he had collected personal information from thousands of students who had registered on the newly launched website. Swisher uses this quote to illustrate Zuckerberg's early attitude toward users' data and privacy.

information can then be matched against your Facebook profile where you might have recently updated your status to "Expecting" and your partner's profile showing searches in parenting groups. Combined, this paints an incredibly detailed picture of your life.

3. A data ecosystem without clear boundaries
Facebook has built an extensive network of advertising partners who, under certain conditions, can gain access to the collected data. This creates an ecosystem that is both complex and difficult to oversee. Through tools like Custom Audiences, advertisers upload customer lists to find matching Facebook users, while Lookalike Audiences use that data to find similar potential customers.

For example, a company selling baby products can use data from the Facebook pixel to identify people who have recently shown interest in pregnancy and parenthood. They can then find other users who behave similarly and target them with highly relevant ads. These insights make it possible for advertisers— and sometimes their partners within Meta's platform—to combine information and create highly specific target groups.

Needless to say, the Facebook pixel a powerful tool for marketers, while simultaneously raising serious questions about data protection.

A systemic problem

The Swedish pharmacy case is not unique. When Swedish Radio began investigating pharmacies sharing data with Facebook, similar issues were soon identified at other pharmacies across Europe, particularly in Norway. While Sweden grappled with the fallout of its pharmacy scandal, Denmark took a broader approach to assess the extent of online tracking, the unclear allocation of responsibility, and the lack of transparency in the digital ecosystem. To address this, the Danish Agency for Digital Government—the authority tasked with enforcing the ePrivacy Directive—conducted a comprehensive review of the country's largest websites in 2023.

How Data Flows to Alphabet

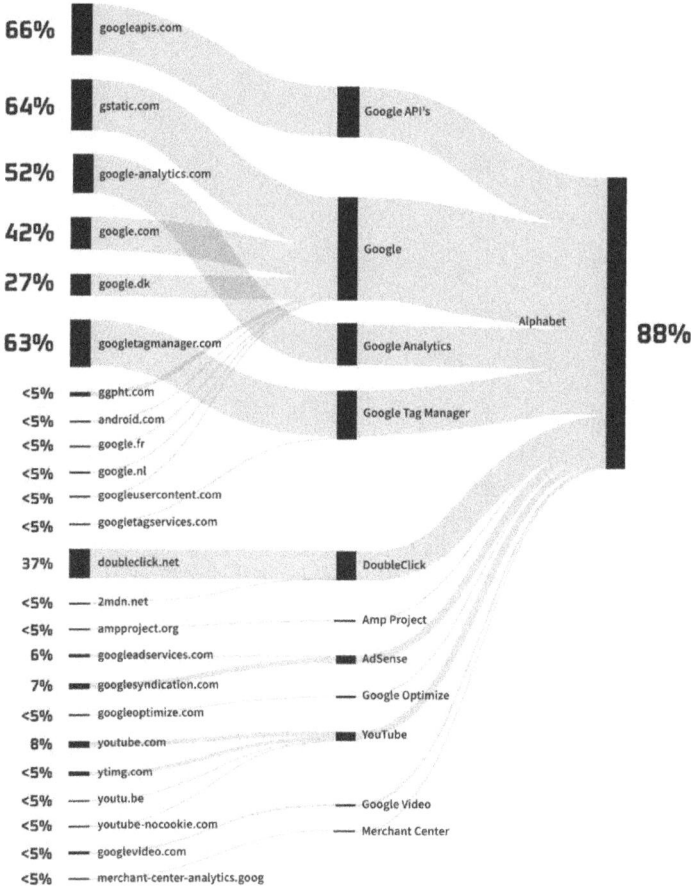

The relationship between third-party domains and third-party services owned by Alphabet, e.g. Google Analytics, YouTube, AdSense. Source: The Danish Agency for Digital Government, Denmark, September 2023.

How data flows to Meta

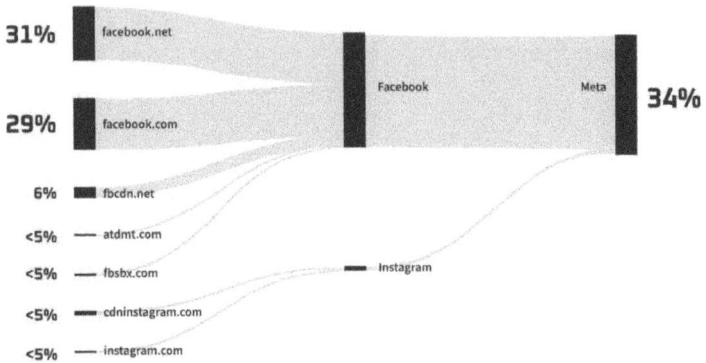

31% facebook.net

29% facebook.com

6% fbcdn.net

<5% atdmt.com

<5% fbsbx.com

<5% cdninstagram.com

<5% instagram.com

Facebook

Instagram

Meta **34%**

Here we see the relationship between third-party domains and third-party services owned by Meta. Source: The Danish Agency for Digital Government, Denmark, September 2023.

The findings of the Danish investigation were striking. The analysis revealed that 98 percent of the 11,137 most visited Danish websites used at least one third-party service, meaning data about visitors was routinely shared with external parties. This led the Danish Agency for Digital Government to conclude that it is highly unlikely such widespread data sharing could be based on valid user consent, given the scale and opacity of these practices.

The mapping also revealed a digital infrastructure dominated by a few major players. Google was present on 88 percent of the websites, Facebook on 34 percent. In addition, the study showed that 93 percent of the websites used services from the United States, raising questions about how European data flows into American jurisdiction.

When the GDPR is not sufficiently leveraged

The Danish investigation confirms what the pharmacy cases implies: the Facebook pixel is more than just a technical tool for web analytics. It is a symptom of a broader problem—a digital ecosystem dominated by a handful of tech giants, whose incentive is to collect and analyze data in ways that far exceed what most users and website owners realize or can control.

So why has Europe not been able to rein in on these systematic data transfers? Some would point at the main supervisory authority responsible for enforcing the GDPR against the big tech players, the Irish Data Protection Commission (DPC). As discussed, every EU country has its own data protection authority responsible for ensuring GDPR compliance. However, under the "one-stop-shop" mechanism of the GDPR, companies doing business across the EU are required to deal primarily with the data protection authority in the country where they have their main European office. Since many large tech companies—including Facebook and Google—have chosen to base their EU headquarters in Ireland, the DPC is the main regulator for these companies, even when it comes to data processing affecting users in other EU countries.

This arrangement has created several concerns. First, many authorities lack the staff and resources needed to conduct the in-depth, complex investigations required to tackle these tech giants. Second, Ireland has a strong economic incentive to keep these companies in the country, which has led to less rigorous oversight.

This is one reason why EU lawmakers have introduced powerful new regulations like the Digital Markets Act (DMA) and Digital Services Act (DSA). While the GDPR mandates consent and transparency, it does not address the underlying power imbalance that allows companies like Facebook to develop tools so complex that both users and regulators struggle to scrutinize them. Moreover, for the DMA at least, oversight is centralized under the European Commission rather than left to the data protection authorities of the individual member states.

So no, the pixel is not tastier than the cookie or other cookie-placing scripts—it is baked from the same problematic recipe.

10. Cookie-banner fatigue?

Misplaced indignation.

Is the cookie banner an annoying phenomenon? The box that pops up on every other website you visit, asking you to take a stance on cookies and tracking. It is often designed to get you to click "Accept All"—the big green or blue button—while "Reject" or "Customize Settings" are less prominent or buried a layer deeper.

In May 2023, when Google announced that anyone who wanted to display ads on their sites through Google's ad-tech system must have a proper banner, the cookie pop-up became a million-dollar question. But what exactly constitutes a proper banner? And why does Google care?

To understand this, we first need to step back and look at what a cookie banner is—and what it is not. Even though we all encounter them daily, surprisingly few people know what a cookie banner is supposed to do, or that it represents a legal contract between the website and the visitor.

First and foremost, a cookie banner is not an information box telling you the website uses cookies. It is a tool for concisely and clearly requesting user consent before tracking begins. If a visitor declines cookies and tracking, the website must respect that choice and block the scripts that place the cookies. It is also not permitted to have only a "yes, please" or "I understand" button without a "no thanks" option on the first layer of the banner.

Only two of eight political parties followed the law

In August 2022, just a couple of weeks before general election in Sweden, I audited the websites of the country's eight parliamentary parties to see how they handled cookies and user consent. The results were that only two of the eight parties came close to following the regulations. One party even placed cookies before consent was given and continued tracking visitors after they had explicitly declined. Another party shared data with third parties without informing visitors.

The most common violations were making it harder to reject cookies than to accept them, failing to specify how long cookies would be stored, and making it impossible to withdraw previously given consent. One party had a completely dysfunctional cookie banner where all cookies were placed regardless of what the visitor chose. When this was discovered, the party in question removed the banner and all the services that placed cookies, but left behind a cookie policy that listed and described cookies the site no longer used.

That political parties fall short in respecting visitors' data protection rights, is particularly striking. After all, this concerns every citizen's fundamental right not to be tracked against their will—a right that is rarely more crucial than during an election campaign. At the same time, I have great sympathy for the web editors of the parties, who likely felt as comfortable with GDPR and online tracking as I did before I started working on these issues full-time.

EDPB states the dos and do nots

One could state that cookie banners have become the wild west of user interfaces. Some are legitimate attempts at compliance, others are masterclasses in manipulation, designed to trick users into clicking "Accept All" while burying the "Reject" option so deep you would need a mining permit to find it.

But some kind of breaking point arrived in 2021 when the privacy organization NOYB (None of Your Business) launched a campaign aiming to scan up to 10,000 of the most visited websites in Europe for deceptive cookie banners. In their first wave, they sent over 500 draft complaints to companies using non-compliant banners, giving them a one-month grace period to fix the matter. According to NOYB, about 42 percent of the violations were remedied after this warning step. For the remaining cases, NOYB filed 422 formal complaints with data protection authorities across Europe.[61] This large-scale enforcement effort led the European Data Protection Board (EDPB) to set up a Cookie Banner Taskforce, which held 13 meetings between May 2021 and August 2022 to analyze the complaints and review industry practices.

The resulting EDPB report[62] emphasized several key requirements for cookie banners:

o Users must be able to reject cookies as easily as they can accept them.
o The "Reject" option should be as visible and accessible as the "Accept All" button; it should not be hidden behind additional clicks or presented in a less prominent way.
o Cookie banners must not use pre-selected options (such as pre-ticked boxes), and designs must not manipulate users into making a particular choice.

These positions build on earlier EDPB guidance, like the May 2020 guidelines[63] on consent under the GDPR, which set high standards for what constitutes valid user agreement. And in November 2023, the EDPB adopted further guidelines[64]

---

[61] NOYB, "Noyb files 422 formal GDPR complaints on nerve-wrecking cookie banners," NOYB, August 10, 2022, https://noyb.eu/en/noyb-files-422-formal-gdpr-complaints-nerve-wrecking-cookie-banners (accessed July 8, 2025).
[62] European Data Protection Board, "Report of the work undertaken by the Cookie Banner Taskforce," January 18, 2023, https://www.edpb.europa.eu/our-work-tools/our-documents/other/report-work-undertaken-cookie-banner-taskforce_en.
[63] European Data Protection Board, "Guidelines 05/2020 on consent under Regulation 2016/679," May 4, 2020, https://www.edpb.europa.eu/sites/default/files/files/file1/edpb_guidelines_202005_consent_en.pdf (accessed July 8, 2025).
[64] European Data Protection Board, "Guidelines 2/2023 on the technical scope of Article 5(3) of the ePrivacy Directive," November 2023,

clarifying that the rules on consent and user choice apply not only to traditional cookies but also to a broader range of tracking technologies.

What cookies does your website place on visitors' browsers? Here is how to do a simple check:

Step-by-Step

1. Close all browser windows
2. Open a new incognito window (Ctrl+Shift+N)
3. Visit the website
4. Right-click and select "Inspect"
5. Go to the "Application" or "Storage" tab*
6. Expand "Cookies"
7. Click on the domain name for detailed information

What you will see: Cookie name, value, domain, expiration date

Pro tips: Incognito mode provides a clean slate for initial testing. Compare results across different browsers. Check the website's cookie policy, if they have one, and compare.

Different browsers: handle cookies in different ways. Chrome, Firefox, and Safari offer varying levels of cookie control, from blocking third-party cookies to preventing cross-site tracking. It is worth testing your website across multiple browsers.

*The Inspect-option opens the Developer Tools, where the "Application" tab is specific to Chrome and Edge; Firefox uses "Storage," and Safari calls it "Storage" inside the Web Inspector.

---

https://edpb.europa.eu/our-work-tools/our-documents/guidelines/guidelines-22023-technical-scope-art-53-eprivacy-directive_en (accessed July 8, 2025).

While the report of the EDPB reflects a strong consensus among European regulators, some specific details, such as exact button colors or contrast, may still be interpreted differently at the national level. Nonetheless, the overall direction is clear: Cookie banners must offer genuine, user-friendly choices and avoid manipulative design.

When the ad-tech industry tried to set its own consent standards

When the GDPR was set to take effect in 2018, the ad-tech industry faced a massive challenge: How do you handle consent requirements in a world in which hundreds of different players are involved in every single ad impression?

The industry trade group IAB Europe attempted to solve this by launching the Transparency & Consent Framework (TCF) on April 25, 2018, a system for how consent would be managed and shared among various players in the digital advertising chain.

TCF quickly became a recognized standard that many companies adopted, particularly through consent platforms like Cookiebot and Cookie Information, which integrated support for IAB's framework into their solutions so website owners could implement TCF-compatible consent banners. But problems emerged as early as in 2019.

Following 22 complaints, the Belgian data protection authority launched an investigation into the framework. In February 2022, the final verdict arrived: TCF violated the GDPR on multiple fronts. Most critically, the framework did not give users sufficient control over their data. Additionally, the authority determined that IAB Europe itself was acting as a joint data controller for all data passing through the system— something the organization absolutely did not want to accept.

While IAB's framework is not easy to understand (the devil is in the details here too), it is easy to see why they would not want responsibility for how personal data gets handled throughout the system. It is one thing for an individual website owner to be legally responsible for personal data they collect through, say, a CRM system. But becoming responsible for how personal data is handled by every actor using a system you developed? That is suddenly a much scarier territory.

But the Belgian data protection authority (APD) was clear in their reasoning. They emphasized that since the IAB had developed the consent string that forms the backbone of the TCF, they played a decisive role in determining what this data string would be used for and how. Not only did they determine its purpose, they also controlled how it was generated, modified, and read, as well as how and where necessary cookies were stored. Furthermore, it was IAB Europe that decided who would receive the personal data and on what grounds storage periods for the TCF strings would be established.

Yes, IAB Europe appealed the decision.

And yes, the Court of Justice of the European Union issued a preliminary ruling on March 7, 2024, that the TC string, especially when linked to an IP address, constitutes personal data.

The court further specified that IAB Europe should be considered jointly responsible as a data controller for creating and using the TC string within the TCF system. This means IAB, together with its members, bears legal responsibility.

Note that when the EU court says "members," they do not just mean website owners using the framework, but everyone in the digital advertising ecosystem who participates in the string—publishers, e-commerce companies, marketing agencies, various intermediaries, national IAB organizations, ad-tech players who profit from ad space on websites or in apps. So yes, it includes companies like Google, Meta, Microsoft, The Trade Desk, RTL, GroupM, and Publicis.

This broad definition of responsibility became even more consequential with the ruling of the Brussels Court of Appeal in May 2025. The court confirmed that the TC string is personal data and that IAB Europe, together with all TCF participants, are jointly responsible for how this data is created and used within the framework. However, the court clarified that the responsibility of IAB Europe does not extend to all downstream processing for advertising purposes. On the contrary, its joint controllership is limited to the creation and use of the TC string itself. The ruling also reaffirmed that the TCF, in its current form, fails to meet key GDPR requirements, forcing the industry to address these shortcomings as soon as possible. So, while the court did not outright ban the use of the TCF, it did make it clear that, in its current form, the framework does not meet GDPR standards. As a result, IAB Europe and all participants must update their practices and the TCF itself to achieve compliance—meaning significant changes are now unavoidable for anyone relying on the framework.

More on the TCF in upcoming chapters. Now, it is time to take a look at how Google has been maneuvering in parallel to the TCF-story.

Google's take on consent

In September 2020, as regulatory scrutiny of online consent practices was intensifying across Europe, Google launched the first version of Consent Mode (v1). This was Google's way of helping website owners and advertisers using tools like Google Analytics and Google Ads to navigate the increasingly complex landscape of consent regulations.

Three years later, in November 2023, the next step materialized: Consent Mode v2.

So why is Google investing so much time and money in consent issues, really?

What is a consent management platform, and why does Google care?

A Consent Management Platform, or CMP, is, as we have touched upon, much more than just the banner you see popping up on websites. Under the hood lies a complex system that:

1. Scans the website to identify scripts and cookies in use, typically through automated detection but sometimes complemented through manual review, essentially mapping all the technical components that collect or store user data in any way.
2. Categorizes these scripts and cookies by purpose (necessary, analytics, marketing).
3. Creates a registry of all visitor consents, keeping track of who said yes and no to what.
4. Most crucially—blocks or activates scripts based on the visitor's choices, and ensures these preferences get communicated to third-party services like Google Analytics or Facebook.

When a visitor lands on a website for the first time, several events happen simultaneously. The CMP blocks all non-essential scripts, the banner appears with choice options, and when the visitor makes their choice, this gets saved as a "consent string"—a code containing information about exactly what the user accepted or rejected. The consent is then communicated to all relevant services on the site.

This is where Google Consent Mode enters the picture. Consent Mode is an API. To understand why it seems crucial for Google, we need to break down how it works.

A translator between the consent platform and Google's services

Think of Consent Mode as a messenger that carries notes between your cookie banner and Google's tools. Here is why that matters: When someone visits a website that uses Google Analytics or Google Ads, the tools need to know whether they have permission to track that visitor.

Without Consent Mode, every website would have to figure out their own way to tell Google "this person said yes" or "this person said no." So what is Google's solution? They created a standardized messaging system through Consent Mode. But here is the catch: This convenient little messenger only talks to Google's services, not anyone else's.

The first version of Consent Mode (v1) could handle two types of signals whether the visitor had accepted

1. analytics cookies (analytics_storage)
2. and marketing cookies (ad_storage).

But in the fall 2023, Google launched version 2 of Consent Mode, which introduced two new signals specifically for advertising:

3. ad_user_data (for collecting data about the user),
4. and ad_personalization (for personalized ads).

But with Consent Mode v2, Google seems to take the art of keeping your cake and eating it too to an entirely new level.

Now each website can choose to run consent mode in either basic version or advanced version. In basic mode, it is straightforward: If the visitor says no to tracking, no data gets collected. But in advanced mode, something else happens. Here Google sends what they call "cookieless pings," which allow them to collect small data points even from visitors who will decline tracking, because the collection happens before they have clicked yes or no on the cookie banner.

Google tries to justify this by saying that these "pings" only contain, limited information, such as device type, conversion event, time of day, and country. Google claims these data are "non-identifying" and are used exclusively in aggregate to improve conversion modeling.

Alexander Hanff (LLM, CIPPE, CIPT) · 1st (edited) 10mo ···
Internationally Recognised Privacy Technologist, Data Pr...

Advanced Mode is illegal, period. Any access to or storage of information on the terminal equipment of the end user requires consent under Article 5(3) of 2002/58/EC or (in the UK) Regulation 6 of PECR.

The "cookieless ping" they are referring to is a forced connection to their server so they can collect device information such as IP address, User Agent String, Fonts, Operating System and various other information for them to perform fingerprinting and/or compare with data they have from elsewhere. This is outright illegal, as this, without question, requires consent.

One could even argue that this is also a breach of Article 5(1) of 2002/58/EC and Part 2 of the Investigatory Powers Act (a criminal offence) as it could be argued that this forced "cookieless ping" involves an interception of communications without a warrant or consent of all parties.

As such as a company deploying GCM V2 Advanced Mode - you could literally be convicted under criminal law for facilitating that interception.

So in the words of my old mate Harry Callahan: "You've got to ask yourself one question: 'Do I feel lucky?' Well, do you, punk?"

Like · 31 | Reply · 16 Replies

However, from an ePrivacy perspective, whether the data identify or not is beside the point. The ePrivacy Directive applies to any storage of, or access to, information on a user's device regardless of whether the information is personal data[65]. No wonder data protection experts like Alexander Hanff question it emphatically.[66] He is a lawyer, a data protection and cybersecurity expert, and a strategic advisor to the EDPB board, who stress that there is no question that cookieless pings are a big no-no.

So how should ordinary website owners and publishers deal with this?

Google has a monopolistic position within the digital ecosystem. Their tools permeate the entire digital advertising chain: from Google Analytics for web analysis, Google Ads for advertising, Google Ad Manager for publishers, to Ad Exchange where ad space gets bought and sold in real-time. Not to mention YouTube as a video advertising platform and Display & Video 360 for programmatic advertising. This massive ecosystem is so deeply woven into today's digital marketing that it is virtually impossible to avoid.

For marketers and advertisers, this creates an almost unsolvable dilemma: Use Google's tools and you risk violating data protection laws; skip them and you risk losing crucial insights into your digital presence and your ability to effectively reach your target audience.

The situation gets even more complicated because, as discussed, Google now requires anyone using their advertising

---

[65] Conversion modeling is basically the reward for using Consent Mode. (If you do not use it, you get punished by losing your data and thus your ability to act on it = optimize your ads.) Google offers website owners a way to gain insights into how their ads are performing even when a large portion of visitors have declined marketing and analytics cookies.

[66] Alexander Hanff. Advanced Mode is Illegal, published as a comment on Tash Whitaker's post about Consent Mode v2, February 9, 2024: https://www.linkedin.com/feed/update/urn:li:activity:7161726353099210753/

system to implement a certified CMP with Consent Mode v2. Is there an alternative? Would you want to lose access to valuable data from both analytics and advertising? This has created an interesting market dynamic where CMP providers like Cookie Information and Cookiebot get rewarded by Google to integrate Consent Mode into their platforms while simultaneously getting an influx of new customers, who must use their services to keep using Google's tools. It is an alliance that might make economic sense for all parties involved, but it turns CMP providers into what can best be described as neutral bystanders in the larger debate about data protection and privacy online.

That last point is crucial to keep in mind. No matter which tools you choose—even a CMP that builds its entire business model around current data protection laws—you are the one who bears legal responsibility for the tools you decide to use.

For anyone wanting to run successful marketing with a privacy-first perspective, the situation seems almost insurmountable. How do you navigate an ecosystem dominated by players whose business models rely on extensive data collection and profiling? It is a question that demands both new ways of thinking and concrete tools—something we will explore more closely in upcoming chapters, not least through conversations with some of the industry's most compelling voices.

IV

Digital
Advertising

11. Ad fatigue

The marketplace nobody trusts.

We have now seen how the web as a marketplace runs on cookies, pixels, and personal data. But what does this technical infrastructure mean for the people it affects? It is hard not to answer: a fundamental erosion of trust, which is poisoning the entire digital economy.

If data is the new oil (remember when it felt important, profound, and trendy to point that out?), then cookies and pixels are the pipelines that transport it. The largest biggest diesel-powered vessels in this digital oil economy are undoubtedly Alphabet and Meta, though smaller independent ad-tech ships also sail with considerable speed across the sea we call the World Wide Web. Together, they generate astronomical sums from access to what has long been considered "free" data—or at least from the illusion that personal data is free to exploit.

"But a little advertising in exchange for personal information is not so bad, is it?" someone might object. "Even if we're getting ad fatigue?"

It depends. When advertising is based on your sexual orientation, ethnicity, health condition, or what medications you have purchased, the question immediately becomes more complex. What is acceptable for one person to receive targeted ads about can be deeply problematic for another.

Today's situation is particularly troubling because closed platforms like Facebook ("walled gardens") and open ad-tech systems decide what you should see based on information you might not even know they have. And when these systems can influence what political advertising you are exposed to during an election campaign, the democratic implications become urgent.

Meanwhile, the effectiveness of targeted advertising has lured advertisers away from traditional journalistic media. Since the early 2000s, we have witnessed a dramatic shift of advertising revenue to digital intermediaries, creating existential challenges for many newspapers. "The death of newspapers" became a real phenomenon. In bitter irony, the very publishers who produce the content, have become dependent on tech companies for distribution and advertising revenue—a codependency, which threatens the foundation of a free press.

To understand the way forward, we will meet three voices in the coming chapters, who show alternative paths in different ways:

- o Korzeniowski, whose work with Piwik PRO demonstrates how web analytics can function without the surveillance we have described in previous chapters.
- o Arielle Garcia, who reveals from inside the ad-tech industry how the technical systems we have examined are used to circumvent users' rights.
- o Erik Bugge, who proves through Kobler that effective digital advertising is possible without the extensive data collection we have mapped out.

Their perspectives do not only provide deeper understanding of how today's digital advertising landscape works. They also show what tomorrow's privacy-first marketing could look like. As with oil, the costs—both economic and societal—have become too high. It is overdue to explore alternative energy sources for the digital economy.

12. The reformed ad-tech addict?

"IAB's TCF framework is a scam."

"Someone in the industry put it perfectly. He said it is pretty depressing that in the 1960s, the brightest minds built rockets that could take us to the moon. This century, they're building ad-tech solutions," says Piotr Korzeniowski and pauses, then adds.

"That statement is at least partially true."

He should know.

Korzeniowski teaches internet marketing at Kozminski University in Warsaw, served as CEO of Piwik PRO[67] and was instrumental in scaling Clear Code, which builds marketing and ad-tech solutions for an industry that he now describes as "not exactly brimming with people who have good intentions."

"But I say that with a major caveat, he quickly adds. "Not everyone in ad-tech is bad. I've worked with many fantastic clients who I'm still in touch with, and they're genuinely wonderful people. They understand what privacy means and they respect it."

Korzeniowski does not want his criticism of the ad-tech industry to be seen as a criticism that developed gradually, or even as stemming from the fact that he now represents a privacy-focused company that long positioned itself as "the perfect alternative to Google Analytics." From day one, he could describe the interpersonal culture in the industry as intrusive by nature, with little respect for people's privacy—online or offline—though with some shining exceptions.

"I particularly remember an American platform doing business in Europe", he recalls. They looked straight at me and showed how they had a bunch of data points flagged in their

---

[67] The interview with Piotr Korzeniowski was conducted in spring 2023. In spring 2025, he stepped down from his role as CEO of Piwik PRO.

system because users had opted out of retargeting. Then they asked me how they could monetize that data anyway.

"Beyond the shameless disrespect for individuals' right not to be tracked," Korzeniowski continues, "it was confirmation of how toothless IAB's so-called Transparency and Consent Framework really was."[68]

"The whole framework is a scam."

"It was something of a wake-up call to see in black and white how websites using the framework for consent collection were still passing the data along, just with a flag attached. That shouldn't happen in the first place. A 'no' is not a 'maybe."

For Korzeniowski, activating the TCF framework for the Piwik PRO platform was never on the table.

A recovering dataholic?

Personal data—often highly sensitive—is the high-octane fuel that powers the ad-tech and mar-tech industries. Korzeniowski's previous ventures delivered software and systems for this very industry, including platforms for both the supply and demand side of digital advertising.

How does he view his past? Does Korzeniowski see himself as a recovering dataholic?

"I would probably call myself more of a "former ad-tech addict," he says with a wry smile.

"Of course I look back at that industry with strong skepticism, since I now help marketers from the opposite side—with privacy tech."

Does the ad-tech industry have a future?

"I would have loved for the industry to go completely contextual—completely anonymous and tracking-free. Where visitors get served ads that fit the context based on machine learning. For example, someone reading an article about hybrid

---

[68] See chapter 12 "Cookie-banner fatigue?"

cars gets an ad for a particular engine. And the ad only appears after the visitor has actually read the content on the page."

The concept Korzeniowski describes is the polar opposite of how targeted advertising and retargeting work today, where companies track and single out individuals based on what they have looked at before. There are extremely effective platforms for contextual marketing today. But when I ask why the entire industry could not shift to contextual solutions, he shakes his head.

"I think that is wishful thinking. It would require a global transformation that I just do not see as possible right now," he explains, pointing to the situation in the United States.

"At the federal level, they could—or maybe will—break up Google or Alphabet into smaller pieces to increase market competition, just like they did with Standard Oil[69]. But even if they do that, it won't be the death knell for tactical real-time bidding, fingerprinting, and all the rest," Korzeniowski says.[70]

"Unfortunately."

A cat-and-mouse game

Korzeniowski describes the battle between ad-weary consumers and profit-hungry advertisers as an endless cat-and-mouse game. In the first round, aggressive online advertising led to ad-blockers. People got fed up with invasive ads, and solutions to combat them found a strong market, which meant that, in the short term, we escaped those pop-ups that jumped out at us, Korzeniowski explains. But when apps and cell phones became the next big thing, the hunt for consumers moved there.

"Today, they're inside your connected TV. You'd be amazed if you knew how many ad-trackers are running on those

---

[69] Standard Oil was a controversial American oil company with monopoly status. In 1911, the U.S. government broke up the company into 34 separate entities.

devices," Korzeniowski says, describing the constant drive to find new channels and data sources.

Korzeniowski seems to suggest that as long as there is money to be made from advertisers, the incentive persists to circumvent each new blocking mechanism in their respective ecosystems while simultaneously hunting for fresh opportunities in other interfaces. The global ad-tech market was estimated at $783.46 billion[71] in 2023. This figure is comparable to the entire GDP of countries like Sweden or Belgium, underscoring just how significant this sector has become in the global economy.

Money is not the only driving force, though. Korzeniowski believes the brightest physicists, mathematicians, and statisticians are working in ad-tech today. And for them, he explains, it is enormously stimulating to tackle fascinating mathematical challenges within ad-tech, since there is probably no other field that generates such massive amounts of data.

"And you actually can build genuinely useful ad-tech solutions. If you are, say, a major global B2C publisher with a strong brand, you can build solutions that offer real value to your customers," he says, describing how you might map visitors' locations with areas that have higher credit ratings to offer better terms.

The example raises some ethical questions and must be built on informed, transparent consent, but the point of Korzeniowski's example is the importance of being relevant as

---

[71] The cited figure for the ad-tech market's revenue in 2023, amounting to $783.46 billion, is based on a report from Fortune Business Insights, which documents the growth of the market and expects it to reach $2.547 trillion by 2032. It is important to note that different estimates exist for the size of the ad-tech market. These differences stem from varying methodologies and definitions of what is included in "revenue" or "net worth." Revenue typically refers to total income from sales of services and products, while net worth may include other financial aspects such as costs and debt. This makes it challenging to establish an exact figure, resulting in multiple estimates from different sources. https://www.fortunebusinessinsights.com/adtech-market-110325

a marketer. He explains how many solutions often lack any sensible "frequency capping", which is why you can easily become overexposed to a targeted ad.

A major downside of today's ad-tech is how it has "polluted" the web with ads for products customers have already purchased or based on assumptions that lead to wrong conclusions about potential buyers. In other words, they are solutions that, reveal that the smartest minds are not always behind the controls. Or that not everyone cares about elegance.

"They offer hyper-personalized advertising. But that is not true. They just shovel personal data down the supply chain and hope that each ad gets exposed to thousands of people to generate a few clicks," he claims.

In any case, this situation has led to technical countermeasures like ad-blockers, which are then circumvented. Cat. Mouse. Etc. The process is damaging to brands that want to build trust. And it is simply not good for the web as a marketplace or public square.

"I am convinced, though, that it is not so much pressure from lawmakers as changes in browsers that will force the advertising market to change," says Korzeniowski.

Even though laws, industry players, and people's attitudes toward their privacy are correlated forces, it is primarily the phase-out of third-party cookies and other browser restrictions that represent the egg in the "chicken or egg equation," is Korzeniowski argument. He continues.

"Browser restrictions have no national borders. They apply globally. You can pass national laws, but not global ones. And the industry won't regulate itself either, despite what IAB often claims."

But more restrictive browsers also have undesirable consequences. Korzeniowski points out how they can degrade various useful and legitimate site functions like chatbots and web analytics. He also highlights the inconvenience that there is no standard across all browsers. Pointing at how Safari and Firefox are ahead on privacy protection issues, while the big dominant player, Chrome, with more than 60 percent of the global browser market, has been trying to develop supposedly privacy-friendly cookie replacements, which of course are not particularly privacy-friendly at all.

"With the Topics API, Chrome stores some information about you in the browser that tracks which pages you have recently visited. If you have looked at a page about cars and another about ping-pong balls, you might get ads targeted to you based on these topics when you visit, say, the Wall Street Journal, which also uses the Topics API," he explains.

"But this is not how it should be. A browser is not supposed to be an advertising product, for crying out loud!" he retorts.

Can companies rise above this cat-and-mouse game?

Top three tips for going privacy-first

"My first piece of advice is no half-measures. Go all in."

What Korzeniowski's getting at is simple: Replace any service providers on your website that do not cut it from a privacy perspective. If you cannot dump them, you need to document your reasoning. Have you tried getting your vendors to change their ways? Stay on top of things by putting internal processes in place for how things get implemented, swapped out, and managed.

"When you take the leap and prioritize privacy, people will start asking tough questions if you are not being consistent about it," Korzeniowski says and explains how Piwik PRO caught heat for hosting their website in the United States, which prompted them to quickly move it to Swedish servers. He says that if you try to cut corners or make something appear true when it is not, you may end up with a whistleblower in your own ranks.

"Number two: You do not have to go it alone. Privacy is not expensive. But you might hit resistance from the marketing team. That is why you need someone who can bridge that gap, a

DPO, for instance. Marketing cannot operate in a bubble, nothing changes that way, he points out and continues.

"And number three: Realize you do not need nearly as much data as you think. Less is more. No marketer wants to lose data. But at the end of the day, it is about conversions. The goal is to optimize for what actually moves the needle. Optimize for impact, not volume."

But are there examples of successful privacy-first marketing?

The naked blogger

Korzeniowski believes there are plenty of good examples of privacy-first marketing. But the story he shares is one that may seem hard-core.

"We have a blogger in Poland who writes about personal finance. He has millions of followers. Basically, every tenth Pole knows who he is. Two years after the GDPR, he decided to strip his entire website bare. He removed everything. No tracking cookies, no chatbots, no third-party tools. His site became a digital minimalist," Korzeniowski explains and adds:

"It is simply a self-hosted WordPress blog. Nothing more. And he makes millions every year. His readers know this because he publishes his tax returns on the blog. Talk about transparency."

What does he make money from?
"He has some affiliate links on the site, but the UTM tracking belongs to the affiliate only. He does not know how many people click on them. He only knows they work from the money that hits his bank account," Korzeniowski says, adding:

"He has also written several books that sell incredibly well, which makes sense given that his blog pulled and probably still pulls enormous traffic."

So he does not measure clicks or visits. The only thing he measures his success by is his bank account balance. But what if you cannot and do not want to go that hardcore? What is a good balance between respecting your users' privacy and the need to gather useful data?

Is there a perfect privacy balance?

"Now, I represent a privacy-tech vendor, so take this with a grain of salt. But I believe privacy and data collection cannot go hand in hand. Collecting personal data is inherently invasive. The only thing you can do is try to balance your data needs with each individual's right to privacy. And where that balance point should land depends on the company and the industry."

"At its core," Korzeniowski argues, "it is an uncomfortable compromise. But you can take a pragmatic approach to it by working with harmless numbers based on the most basic data about your visitors; measurements that are completely allowed without consent."

So you can keep your cake and eat it too?

Korzeniowski explains that you can collect anonymized data where there is no way to identify and re-identify the individuals generating the data. If you do that, the GDPR does not apply to that collection and you do not need consent.

"And this is not something I made up. This is something that both France's data protection authority, CNIL, and the European Data Protection Board endorse. You can fulfill data protection authorities' highest aspirations and get useful statistics without having to ask for informed consent first."

"This is what I mean when I say you can go all in with a privacy-first approach, he says."

Korzeniowski states that Piwik PRO is on the French supervisory authority's (CNIL) list of tools, which can run without consent.[72]

---

[72] While the CNIL allows certain analytics tools like Piwik PRO to operate
without consent if configured strictly for anonymous audience measurement,

"We have customers who are willing to make their marketing department completely blind to all traffic where consent has not been given. For some businesses, a privacy-first approach where you go all-in means exactly this. For others, it is collecting basic statistics without information that can be defined as personal data, either by itself or combined with other information," he explains

This approach, Korzeniowski argues, is something a player like Google cannot offer with any credibility whatsoever.

"Both Google Analytics and Piwik PRO can collect data points that do not require consent. Google calls their solution Consent Mode. We call our version Anonymous Data Tracking, but there are two major differences between them and us," says Korzeniowski, describing how Google, unlike Piwik PRO, collects data and is ultimately an advertising factory.

"Google has an interest in reusing the data they collect for you as a website owner in other parts of their ecosystem. You cannot know that they do not do this."

What Korzeniowski highlights is also reflected in, for example, the decisions that the Swedish supervisory authority (IMY) presented in summer 2023, where four Swedish companies were asked to stop using Google Analytics unless they took technical measures, among other things, that anonymized all data points before they were sent to Google. The decision concerned the transfer of personal data to a third country. Google is an American company, meaning it is based in a third country, for which the EU lacked a so-called adequacy decision at the time of the decision. But the decision also pointed to how problematic the situation becomes when the user

---

this exemption is based on the French interpretation of the ePrivacy Directive and may not apply in other EU countries—which the CNIL also underlines in its guidance: "Please note that this section is relative to the ePrivacy directive and may be subject to national variation. Contact your local data protection agency to know its position." See CNIL, "Sheet n°16: Use analytics on your websites and applications," https://www.cnil.fr/en/sheet-ndeg16-use-analytics-your-websites-and-applications (accessed July 8, 2025).

was logged into their Google account when they visited the audited website. The IMY wrote:

Since the complainant was logged into their Google account during the visit to the Website, Google could still have had the opportunity to obtain information about the logged-in user's visit to the Website. The fact that the complaint does not indicate that personalized ads were displayed does not prevent Google from obtaining information about the logged-in user's visit to the Website.[73]

Thus, Korzeniowski stresses that Piwik PRO has higher credibility than Google Analytics, because its purpose is to provide customers with statistical services where they, Piwik PRO, only retrieve rudimentary information about where the customer came from.

"Then we quickly forget the visitor so they cannot be re-identified, which is something completely different from what Google does," he underlines.

Korzeniowski explains that the way Piwik PRO is built, allows users to limit the amount of data points and control exactly what type of data they collect, making it possible to comply with the strict requirements of the GDPR around data minimization and purpose limitation. The tool is simply designed so that the user can find and justify the perfect balance between your visitors' privacy and your data collection.

Piwik PRO's business model is built on offering web analytics tools on the condition that the data remain under the customer's control. But how does the company resist the

---

[73] Swedish Authority for Privacy Protection (IMY), Decision following supervision under the General Data Protection Regulation (GDPR) – CDON AB's transfer of personal data to third countries, case number DI-2020-11397, June 30, 2023, page 14,
https://www.imy.se/globalassets/dokument/beslut/2023/beslut-tillsyn-ga-cdon.pdf

temptation to tap into or examine their customers' data without their consent?

If you have used the product or studied the quote and fine print, the explanation seems obvious. When you buy the platform, you get the key to the house. Piwik PRO does not keep its own set of keys. And if you run the paid version, protection of your data is further strengthened. As a European company, you can then place the platform on servers hosted by a Swedish company in Sweden, for example.

At the same time, there could, at least in theory, be several arguments for Piwik PRO to want to access their customers' statistics.

"Today we know that the web is full of so-called bot traffic, automated web crawlers. It would be interesting to learn how these bots can be detected and excluded from web traffic to improve the quality of analytics data," says Korzeniowski, explaining that they could lean on the legal basis of "legitimate interests" to justify such insight. But they do not want to.

"If this came up, we would first ensure each customer's consent, and we would need to make extensive changes to the terms of use."

Despite the company's platform collecting several billion events per month, they have never tried to build reports for themselves based on that data. That would go against their values and raison d'être, Korzeniowski notes.

And for companies that want to do as much as possible with the data?

Piwik PRO has an integrated consent management platform. In other words, you can ask for informed consent in accordance with legal requirements and your own data-ethical ambitions. For those who want a more permissive privacy balance, this opens up more numbers, but also a bit more "action," so to speak, especially if you activate the customer data platform of the unit.

"You could, for example, set up your website so that it opens a channel to your sales chat for a visitor who has been on the pricing page three times in a row during the last ten minutes. But of course, only if the visitor in question has given their consent for marketing," says Korzeniowski and continuous.
"If consent has not been given, then nothing happens. And that is what makes it beautiful. This is what it looks like in practice when privacy and marketing walk hand in hand."

The original interview with Piotr Korzeniowski was conducted in spring 2023.

13. Browser, browser on the screen

Tell me ...

"I am convinced, though, that it not so much pressure from lawmakers as changes in browsers that will force the advertising market to change," Korzeniowski said in the previous chapter. His observation points to a fascinating paradox in the battle for online privacy—while legislators and regulatory authorities work to control digital surveillance, an equally decisive struggle is playing out in the software we use every day to browse the web.

Browsers have, as Korzeniowski emphasized, no national borders.[74] They are global in reach and central to how the web functions as a marketplace. Despite the rise of apps and especially the recent generative AI explosion, it is still through browsers that we access the open web. They are, as the saying goes, "hiding in plain sight", so fundamental to our daily internet use that we barely reflect on their role. Nevertheless, it is within these seemingly simple programs that much of the battle for our online privacy has been fought in recent years.

As we will see, the struggle is closely intertwined with the commercial interests and power structures we have explored in previous chapters. When Safari and Firefox began blocking third-party cookies it was a direct threat to the surveillance-based business model that dominates today's web. But it was not until Chrome, with its dominant market position, announced the same intentions that the real drama began.

---

[74] This is, of course a truth with modifications, since browsers can be subject to national restrictions in certain countries. In China, for example, browsers such as Safari and Chrome function differently due to restrictions imposed by the one-party state. Because Google services and IP addresses are blocked, Chrome's features are limited, making local search engines the default alternative.

Safari and Firefox took the lead

When Safari introduced its "Intelligent Tracking Prevention" (ITP) in 2017, it was a big deal from a privacy perspective. The ITP is a comprehensive framework that uses machine learning to identify and limit various forms of online tracking.

What does this mean in practice?

Imagine you visit an online store and look at a pair of red Adidas sneakers. With the ITP active in Safari, the store can still see what you do on their site, but they cannot follow you when you move on to browse other websites. This is accomplished through several different protection mechanisms.

First, cookies from the store itself (so-called first-party cookies) are time-limited. Your "profile" on the store gets reset after seven days if you do not return and interact with the site again. In some cases, cookies can even be limited to just one day. Meanwhile, cookies from companies other than the store (the infamous third-party cookies) are blocked entirely. This means advertising companies and other tracking tools cannot follow you between different websites.

The ITP also detects and blocks more sophisticated tracking methods. When you click on a link, for example, ad-tech companies might try to route you through their own websites for a few milliseconds—fast enough that you will not notice but long enough to register your activity. The ITP recognizes and stops these attempts. It also prevents different ad-tech companies from sharing information about your browsing behavior with each other.

Firefox's counterpart to ITP is called Enhanced Tracking Protection (ETP). It is built on a combination of different protection mechanisms. A central component is the use of the Disconnect.me list, which is a registry of known tracking domains that are automatically blocked.

Let us return to our example of the online store and those red Adidas sneakers: With the ETP activated in Firefox, not only are tracking cookies that can follow you between websites (third-party cookies) blocked, but other forms of tracking as well. When the store has a Facebook "Like" button, Facebook can no longer register your visit. Firefox also blocks attempts to identify you through your computer—so-called fingerprinting—and additionally stops hidden cryptocurrency miners that could use your device to generate cryptocurrencies.

Unlike Safari, Firefox also gives you more control over how long cookies can persist. Instead of a fixed seven-day limit, you can decide whether cookies should be cleared when you close the browser or set your own time limits. You can also choose between different protection levels, from standard mode, which blocks the most common tracking methods, to strict mode, which provides maximum protection but may affect how certain websites function.

When Chrome cried wolf

What about the giant Chrome?

With over 60 percent of the global browser market, it is no surprise that Chrome's never-ending attempts (that actually came to an end) to phase out third-party cookies with Privacy Sandbox solutions have had a massive impact on the ad-tech industry.

When Google announced in January 2020 that the days of the third-party cookie were numbered in Chrome, the market reacted immediately. Criteo, one of the world's largest ad-tech companies, saw its market value plummet by 20 percent. This says something about how foundational the concept of tracking (or stalking) individuals online is to the ad-tech economy. Above all, it highlights Google's role as the world's overwhelmingly dominant player in the ad-tech arena. While Safari and Firefox could make their privacy-first decisions from a more straightforward "we-protect-our-users'-privacy" perspective, it was clear that Chrome had to balance (the idea of) a more privacy-friendly approach against Google's own (overriding) business interests. The result, as we have discussed before, was Privacy Sandbox.

But how was this supposed to work?

As we saw in Chapter 10, Privacy Sandbox represented Google's attempt to keep its cake and eat it too. While Safari and Firefox chose to block third-party cookies without fanfare, Google wanted to develop new technical solutions that could enable targeted advertising but in a supposedly more privacy-friendly way. The path toward this end turned out to be much longer and more winding than anyone could have predicted.

In 2023, the industry began testing the new Privacy Sandbox features. Criteo, one of the world's largest ad-tech companies, conducted extensive tests between March and May. But the results were disappointing—neither advertisers nor publishers were largely ready for the transition.

The ad-tech industry was not standing by idly, though. Many stakeholders felt compelled to find new ways to identify and track people on the web. The Trade Desk, one of the largest independent ad-tech companies, took the lead by developing Unified ID 2.0, an attempt to create a new, more transparent standard for the entire industry.

Unlike third-party cookies, which could be placed in users' browsers without their knowledge[75], Unified ID 2.0 was built on a different principle: Users would actively share their email address to receive more "relevant" advertising. The Trade Desk made the solution open source, and other companies like LiveRamp soon came up with their own alternatives.

These new ID solutions combine two types of data: "deterministic" data, which can directly identify you (email address, phone number) and "probabilistic" data (IP address, browser type, screen resolution), details that together can create a digital fingerprint of the user.

On the surface, this seemed like a step forward, identification would become more open and based on active

---

[75] As we saw in Chapter 12, this could happen if the website chose to circumvent its consent management (CMP).

consent. But in practice, the same fundamental problem remained as with third-party cookies: Few users really understood how their information would be used to track them across the internet. It was still the same surveillance-based model, only in new packaging.

Additionally, a new challenge emerged: fragmentation. With multiple competing ID solutions in the market, it became harder for both publishers and advertisers to know which standard to bet on. The Trade Desk had made Unified ID 2.0 open source, but that did not mean everyone wanted to use their particular solution. Several major publishers, like the New York Times, chose not to accept any of the new ID solutions at all, citing user privacy concerns.

Gunning for an industry standard

Google realized they needed more than just technical innovation, they needed legitimacy. As a result, they turned to The World Wide Web Consortium (W3C), the organization that has served as the premier standards body of the web since 1994. Founded by Tim Berners-Lee, the creator of the web itself, W3C has shaped the entire technical foundation that today's web rests on—from HTML and CSS to the protocols that enable browsers to communicate with servers.

Google's decision to seek W3C approval was strategic. If Privacy Sandbox became an official W3C standard, it would essentially force other browsers to implement it, making Google's solution the new norm for targeted advertising across the web.

But W3C's technical committees were skeptical. The Technical Architecture Group (TAG), one of W3C's most influential bodies, leveled particularly harsh criticism against the proposal for "first-party sets"[76]. They described it as outright "harmful to the web in its current form."

---

[76] This was yet another component of the Privacy Sandbox initiative, beyond the APIs we discussed in Chapter 10.

First-Party Sets, which Google later rebranded as *Related Website Sets*, would have allowed companies to declare multiple domains as "one entity." For example, Google could have defined google.com, youtube.com, and doubleclick.net as one and the same "first party." This would have enabled these websites to share data with each other as if they belonged to the same domain.

TAG saw the proposal as an attempt to circumvent the privacy boundaries built into the architecture of the web. It would have blurred the crucial distinction between first and third parties, a distinction that has been central to users' ability to control their data online. Even more troubling, it could have placed even more power in the hands of tech giants, where power is already concentrated.

When W3C refused to grant its blessing, Google chose to forge ahead on its own. While W3C has no formal power to stop a company from implementing new technology, the rejection sent a clear signal: Privacy Sandbox risked undermining the principles of openness and decentralization, which the web was built upon.

Google's decision to proceed anyway raised concerns among several stakeholders, including the British Competition and Markets Authority (CMA), which since January 2021 had been formally assessing whether Privacy Sandbox was compatible with British competition law.

As discussed in Chapter 10, the CMA, which had previously scrutinized Google's dominance in the ad-tech market, saw an imminent risk that the initiative would strengthen Google's already maxed-out position and make it even harder for other players to compete. But the concerns of the CMA were not just about competition. They investigated Privacy Sandbox in consultation with the British data protection authority, the Information Commissioner's Office (ICO), to ensure it met standards from both an antitrust and a privacy perspective.

As we explored in Chapter 10, the CMA had been conducting a comprehensive review of Privacy Sandbox since

2021. What made their W3C rejection particularly significant was its timing, it came amid this ongoing regulatory scrutiny. While Google had been working closely with the CMA throughout the process, making adjustments and counterproposals to address competition concerns, the technical rejection of the W3C added another layer of legitimacy problems to an already complex approval process.

Google initially seemed confident they could navigate both the technical and regulatory hurdles. But as we saw, that confidence would prove misplaced when the CMA ultimately forced Google to abandon the third-party cookie phase-out entirely in July 2024:

We are proposing an updated approach that elevates user choice. Instead of deprecating third-party cookies, we would introduce a new experience in Chrome that lets people make an informed choice that applies across their web browsing, and they'd be able to adjust that choice at any time.

—Anthony Chavez, VP of Google Privacy Sandbox, July 2024

What does this mean for the web?

In many ways, Google's decision to indefinitely pause the phase-out of third-party cookies marks, as discussed already, a fairly dramatic shift in the cookie death narrative. They are not saying goodbye to third-party cookies, but they are also not leaving everything exactly as it has always been. Instead, they are saying that each user should have access to make an active decision about their own data sharing at the browser level.

This has created a pile-up of follow-up questions.

First, what will this "informed choice" look like in practice? Google has been sparse with details, creating uncertainty in the industry. Second, how will this affect existing consent management platforms and their role?

IAB Europe and other industry stakeholders in ad-tech have expressed strong concerns, officially about whether a browser-level consent solution can truly meet GDPR requirements. But where the shoe really pinches for them is probably: What happens if all Chrome users can easily block all third-party tracking? Such a scenario could strangle the business model of the tracking-based ad-tech industry overnight.

But is Google not essentially shooting itself in the foot then?

All else being equal, the answer is no. Since Google is a "walled garden" with enormous amounts of first-party data, Google sits on all its ad-tech platforms plus YouTube with massive amounts of first-party data and is therefore not as vulnerable to changes in third-party tracking as smaller ad-tech players.

But all else is not equal. Google is under heavy antitrust pressure from multiple directions. In Europe, oversight from the DMA is mounting on top of the antitrust lawsuits in the U.S. From this perspective, the Privacy Sandbox retreat can be viewed as a strategic repositioning.

And this is where the story takes a fascinating turn as 2024 was undeniably an eventful year for Google.

During one of the US lawsuits against the company, it emerged that Apple, with its high-minded stance on privacy issues (partly, but not solely, due to Safari's ITP), was simultaneously helping to cement Google's dominance over the digital advertising market. It turned out that Apple annually receives around $20 billion from Google for making their search engine the default in Safari—a sum estimated to represent about 17–18 percent of Apple's profits.[77]

And you know what is even more fascinating?

The lawsuit revealed that the agreement between Apple and Google contained a clause requiring Apple to "support and defend" Google if the US government ever brought antitrust charges against Google. In other words, it is not only about

[77] Bloomberg, "Google's Payments to Apple Reached $20 Billion in 2022, Cue Says," May 2, 2024,
https://www.bloomberg.com/news/articles/2024-05-01/google-s-payments-to-apple-reached-20-billion-in-2022-cue-says

money, but also about active collaboration between tech giants to preserve their respective market positions. You scratch my back, and I scratch yours.

This casts an interesting light on the privacy-on-the-web discourse. While browsers like Safari and Firefox have introduced increasingly strong privacy protections, and Chrome now hesitates before phasing out third-party cookies, the underlying power structures remain intact. It is no longer just about users' right to privacy, but about how this right can be weaponized in the play for market dominance, a dominance that has not only created big fat cats that are no longer particularly innovative but also stifles innovation in a market that could have been so much better than it is.

It is high time for competition regulators in the EU, UK, and U.S. to get a firm grip on the machinations of the tech giants. It is no simple task, however, when the devil is in the details and those details require investigation reports running to hundreds of pages, like the CMA's review of the Privacy Sandbox initiative.

This brings us to Arielle Garcia, whose decision to leave the ad-tech industry was grounded in the realization that the system could not be reformed from within. As she puts it: "… when you keep asking questions but never get answers that make sense, it is because you are not supposed to understand."

14. When big tech derails capitalism

For ten years, Arielle Garcia worked at one of the world's largest media and advertising agencies—UM Worldwide. Successfully, steadily promoted, at the headquarter in New York, until she resigned from her position as *Chief Privacy & Responsibility Officer* in the summer of 2023.

It was not a quiet exit.

Garcia published her decision in an op-ed that appeared in AdExchanger magazine. She acknowledged that leaving UM was not an easy decision, but it was a necessary one. What she was walking away from, she explained, was a business model that had reached the end of the road and an industry incapable of self-examination—one that preferred to walk backwards into the future rather than face hard truths.

Garcia's farewell article went viral.[78]

But what was she really getting at?

Ten years on the agency side gave Garcia what she describes as a heavily buy-side-focused perspective on advertising and ad-tech. She understood the challenges and needs of both agencies and advertisers within the digital advertising ecosystem. But she was not as familiar with the sell-side and publishers' reality. That is why she found the reactions from "the other side" particularly interesting.

"Of course publishers must be incredibly frustrated that agencies just do whatever the big platforms tell them to, and that marketers have such a single-minded focus on cheap reach and low CPMs[79]," Garcia says.

---

[78] Garcia, Arielle. "An Industry in Conflict: It is Time for Tough Questions And Hard Decisions." AdExchanger. Published June 20, 2024. https://www.adexchanger.com/marketers/an-industry-in-conflict-its-time-for-tough-questions-and-hard-decisions/

[79] Cost Per Mille (cost per thousand impressions)

"Publishers, in this dynamic, depend on marketers or agencies demanding quality media. When that demand disappears, the market for quality journalism, for quality publications, gets hollowed out."

What Garcia spotlighted with her departure was how big tech players dictate terms and pocket the lion's share of profits. And that it does not have to be this way.

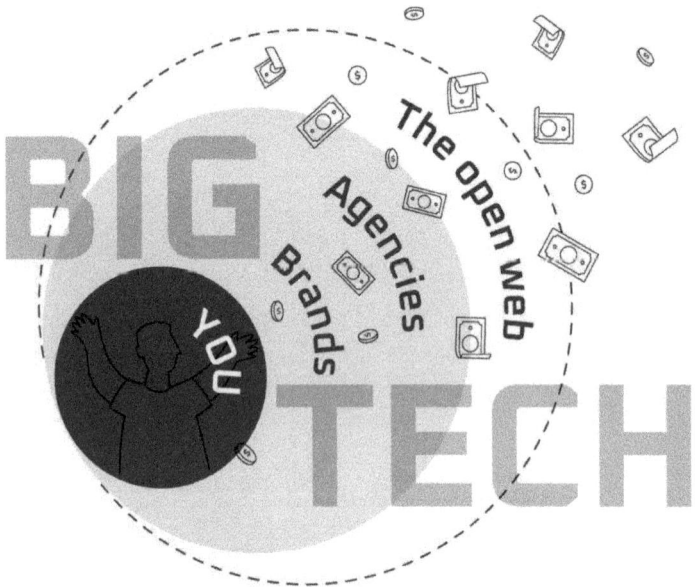

The major tech companies, primarily Meta and Google, operate as *walled gardens* while simultaneously beeing an all-encompassing infrastructure. No one escapes their presence, and the web as a marketplace becomes a less diverse, dynamic, and resilient ecosystem than it could and should be.

Brands pay agencies big money to reach you, the consumer, with advertisements. The agencies themselves execute the bidding and buying through the services and platforms of these big tech companies (as well as through smaller ad-tech players' service platforms). But since these platforms make money per transaction—each ad clicks or impression—there is a built-in corruption mechanism. As an advertiser, you cannot trust that the agency is doing what is best for their clients because they get paid commissions for using and recommending the solutions of the platforms.

"That is the picture you need to understand," Garcia says. "It reveals that the agency a brand hires may have incentives to prioritize short-term strategies that generate more transactions instead of choosing strategies that are more cost-effective and aligned with the brand's long-term goals."

How did the buy-side react?

"They were either glad that someone had finally spoken up and told the truth, or relieved that I had put their concerns into words and made them concrete."

One marketing director wrote to her: "You know, I've always seen how new products from the tech giants show up in my media plans, but I have never understood how they align with our goals. Whenever I raise the issue, I never get an answer." And some told her they had chosen to start their own agencies because they could not create change within the existing system either.

"I expected more pushback"

Garcia had expected more criticism, more people accusing her of being naive and not understanding that "this is just how capitalism works." It is a critique she has little patience for.

"That viewpoint completely misses the point. The system we have grown accustomed to today might look and feel like capitalism, but it is not. It is an oligopoly. A market economy does not function when power is concentrated among so few massive companies," she says, explaining:

"As marketers and agencies, we're living off the scraps that big tech companies throw down to us."

The monopoly

Monopoly is a word Garcia returns to often, especially when talking about Google. As we explored in Chapter 10 with the third-party cookie saga, Google's market dominance creates situations where they can essentially dictate terms for the entire web ecosystem. Since 2020, the U.S. government has sued Google five times for abusing its dominant market position. Today (2025), we have two major concluded cases.

The first concerned Google's search engine, where a federal judge in August 2024 ruled that the company holds an illegal monopoly. The DOJ has demanded that Google's parent company, Alphabet, sell off Chrome entirely and potentially split Android from Google's other products.

The second case focused on Google's role in digital advertising. Eight states together with the Department of Justice argued the company is "three times a monopolist" in digital advertising, controlling every link in the chain worth over $700 billion. In April 2025, another federal judge agreed: Google holds a monopoly in ad-tech too. Needless to say, these cases could finally reshape Google's dominant position in both search and digital advertising.

Garcia describes how this monopolistic situation prevents the digital advertising market from building long-term sustainable business models where companies can take responsibility for where ad dollars go, where ads are displayed, and simultaneously respect people's right to privacy.

"Take the alternative ID solutions, like UID 2.0, for example. They're positioned as alternatives to Google's Privacy Sandbox initiative. Because Google has such a strong position from which they can attract advertisers, these solutions become important for ad-tech companies that want an alternative to Google. But when we zoom out, we see what is really happening is a kind of surveillance arms race among those who make their living collecting massive amounts of personal data for targeted advertising. The situation is harmful to consumers and publishers, but also to marketers," she says, explaining that all these systems force marketers to chase so-called vanity metrics and measure results using misleading and inaccurate attribution models.

Google and Meta are not the whole problem

For Garcia, there is no doubt that the GDPR was an urgently needed legislation. Even though its purpose has been undermined by the lack of strong coherent enforcement.

With the Digital Markets Act (DMA) and Digital Services Act (DSA), the EU is now creating one of the most comprehensive and sophisticated attempts to balance privacy, data protection, and consumer protection with antitrust issues. But if they are going to help fix the situation, enforcement needs to be forceful from the start—and in that regard, not mirror the GDPR track record.

"That could prove difficult," Garcia says, explaining that the giants targeted by the DMA and DSA have the economic resilience to absorb fines and navigate loopholes.

"They can take shelter behind the complexity of their products and the systems they maintain to weather the storms," she notes.

At the same time, Garcia points out that the necessary focus on the big players can overshadow the equally important ecosystem dynamics between the major platforms and media agencies, as well as between advertisers and agencies. To illustrate this, Garcia brings up the Sephora case.

When the French retail chain was fined under the CCPA of California in 2021, it was established that the company had used tracking pixels on its website for advertising purposes. They had collected user data with pixels/cookies, and these data were sent to a platform that enabled Sephora to target ads to individuals. The ruling determined that the data transfer constituted a "sale" of data,[80] and therefore consumers must have the ability to opt out.

Garcia explains that before the Sephora case, many in the industry wanted to argue that such a situation would not count as a "sale." The decision therefore opened the door for media agencies and advertisers to ask uncomfortable follow-up questions of their service providers—like the really big agencies and platforms from Google and Meta. Or at the very least, they became aware that they could and should ask why they had not been informed about such regulatory changes and what risks this carried, since they could now be fined just like Sephora. Undeniably, this could be damaging to the advertiser's reputation and brand.

The Sephora case communicated that there was accountability to be demanded from those who help to measure and execute advertising campaigns. For both advertisers and media agencies, it became harder to be lulled into the false sense of security that Google and Meta tried—and still try—to maintain.

So while the DMA and DSA, and antitrust actions from the U.S. government, put much-needed pressure directly on Google and Meta and other giants, GDPR and GDPR-like decisions (such as those based on the CCPA) against ordinary ad buyers remain important.

---

[80] CCPA defines "sale" of personal information broadly, including data sharing for "valuable consideration" even when no direct monetary transaction occurs. This encompasses using tracking technologies for targeted advertising. A key difference between CCPA and EU regulations is their approach to consent: The GDPR and ePrivacy typically require explicit prior consent (opt-in) before data collection, especially for cookies and tracking technologies. The CCPA instead operates on an opt-out model where companies can collect and use data as long as consumers are given the opportunity to refuse such "sale" of their personal information. This fundamental difference between opt-in and opt-out reflects differing philosophical approaches to data protection in the two regulatory frameworks.

Another example Garcia raises is Meta and the issue of so-called detailed targeting options, which is a feature that made it possible to target ads to people that are based on their health conditions, such as whether someone had diabetes

Today, Meta has reluctantly removed this feature.

First, they implemented a change so that an advertiser could no longer directly target people based on their specific health conditions—like "the person has diabetes." Instead, they offered advertisers the ability to target ads toward related "interests," such as "the person is interested in *World Diabetes Day*," which became a kind of identification by proxy. Eventually, after extensive criticism, Meta chose to phase out the detailed targeting function and replaced it with "custom audiences." This feature allows advertisers to use their own data for targeted ads on Meta's platforms, including sensitive data. The change suggested a shift in responsibility, where Meta essentially said that if the advertiser brought their own data—data that individuals had consented to—then targeted advertising to these audiences could be OK.

"But what message does that send?" Garcia asks rhetorically, continuing:

"So it becomes OK if you bring 'your own data' to the platform?"

After the U.S. Supreme Court struck down Roe v. Wade and gutted women's abortion rights, the question of how hospitals—often unknowingly—send sensitive personal information via pixels to platforms like Meta's Facebook became a hot potato. How could an individual know that their "interest" in medical abortion would not end up in an audience segment? Could this still happen in certain states and jurisdictions but not in other countries?

In response to this, Meta introduced a change in 2023 that they called core setup. With this change, sensitive data and advertisers or campaigns wanting to use sensitive information would be handled in a supposedly more secure way without metadata. But exactly how effectively core setup would protect people's privacy was not crystal clear, so to speak.

"If I'm an advertiser with a website about a particular medication, it doesn't matter how much metadata gets stripped away if the URL is still there," Garcia says.

Garcia is referring to the limitations that metadata removal has from a privacy protection perspective. Even if you remove data points describing where the person is and what time the information was collected, the URL remains. If it is from a website about medicine and a specific disease, this sensitive information gets associated with the individual.

Garcia emphasizes that it is great that the DMA and DSA now place demands on the major platforms, not least by requiring transparency.

"I am looking forward to seeing how companies and advertisers use this transparency to change their own processes and choices," Garcia says, continuing.

"People in their target audiences will, for example, be able to see information about why they are getting a particular ad targeted at them. If you as an advertiser cannot stand behind that information, you are going to question how the platform profiles your leads."

Complex and opaque by design

Garcia started at UM Worldwide as an administrative assistant, and her plan was to keep this simple, stable job while studying for her law degree in the evenings. But after six months, she had been promoted to Global Account Manager, a role she eventually transformed into an operational position. Later it became a combined operational and compliance role. All while she continued her studies.

In law school, Garcia had taken courses in human rights because "privacy was not a thing back then." But the subject was gaining momentum and becoming timely. Soon the Cambridge Analytica scandal broke in 2017. And the year after, the GDPR would take full effect. How would the latter impact e-discovery, one of her professors wondered. E-discovery is the process of identifying, collecting, and analyzing electronic data for use as evidence in legal cases or proceedings.

But while there was at least discussion about the GDPR in her academic program, the attitude at her workplace was a shoulder shrug and a comment like "it'll probably work itself out."

"People weren't worried about what effect the new data protection law in Europe would have on the industry they worked in," Garcia explains "and that was an attitude I strongly opposed, which is why I started taking courses in data protection issues."

While learning everything about the GDPR, she also dove into understanding how ad-tech worked and began applying what was becoming her legal expertise to her work at UM Worldwide. When California developed its own version of the GDPR—the CCPA—she led the entire GDPR work of the organization and was well-prepared.

Anyone who has watched Garcia in the countless interviews she has given, notices that she is substantive in her responses. Garcia is technically versed in the granular details of the ad-tech complex while obviously being legally trained. But she does not want to call herself a quick learner or smarter than anyone else.

"I have an operational background that has made me skilled at figuring out how systems work."

"I absolutely do not understand things right off the bat. It is more that I'm stubborn and won't give up until I reach a conclusion. And sometimes the conclusion is 'This is not clear and transparent. And the reason it is not clear and transparent, is because it has been left unclear on purpose.'"

She explains that one reason for this is that platforms do not want to provide straight answers about how their systems work.

"Take cookies and identifiers, for example, where gaps in clarity and ambiguous design force website owners to realize that every cookie a service provider places can serve multiple purposes." Garcia continues:

"At the same time, vendors keep changing what their products do, which cookies get placed, and what each cookie does."

In other words, mapping a company's data handling is not only complex in itself, but also fluid, and the data environment is dynamic.

"What is true and accurate today is not necessarily true tomorrow," Garcia spells out and continues.

"A situation I'm trying to understand now is how retail media networks function, particularly in terms of how they handle sensitive data."

When I ask Garcia to explain what retail media is, she first laughs and says she almost cannot. But then explains that she is referring to their demand-side platforms (DSPs). These enable them to target ads OUTSIDE their domains using retail data from INSIDE their systems. She gives an American example: Walmart Connect. Walmart is a retail chain that offers everything from groceries to electronics at low prices.

"They operate both online and in physical stores, and as a result have an enormous amount of data about their customers that they can use for targeted advertising. But what I am struggling to understand is how this works when they are no longer just running advertising on their own physical and digital domains. Today there are retail media networks that also help companies outside their own domains," she says.

Garcia is particularly concerned about how these retail networks handle sensitive personal information. They sit on massive amounts of so-called transactional data. The question is how they choose to handle consent requirements, especially when it comes to advertising in the medical field. Garcia points out that this has become an even more pressing issue after the so-called Dobbs decision—the Supreme Court's ruling that eliminated constitutional protection for abortion rights.

"Are advertisers being misled by these networks? Do they think they can avoid ethical and legal consequences despite benefiting from transactional data that has categorized individuals into sensitive cohorts?"

Garcia is referring to the fact that what a company—or in this case, a retail media network—has collected for one purpose cannot simply be used for another, secondary purpose willy-nilly. In the EU, the GDPR requires additional consent from the individuals in question, for example. Garcia thinks this more than reasonable. The restrictions exist to protect consumers' privacy and ensure their data are not used in ways they have not explicitly approved.

"I do not think it is right or reasonable to categorize people into sensitive cohorts. The consumer response won't be positive either. So what I'm prioritizing today is getting answers from these networks. I want to understand what they do with sensitive transactional data."

"Am I going crazy?"

Because ad-tech systems are complex with low transparency and many workarounds, Garcia thinks it is easy to become exhausted.

"Sometimes I wonder if I'm going crazy. It is 2024 and I still see ad-tech companies and data brokers claiming that the data they have is 'de-identified.' And I cannot for the life of me understand in what reality that is true?"

"If you send data to a platform where they take that data and match it against another ID, how in the hell can the data then be 'de-identified'? Do they only hire lawyers who can validate their insane positions? I'm usually good at understanding where the loopholes are or how someone arrived at a conclusion. But this thing does not add up."

To illustrate her point, she raises the question of how the company LiveRamp can match data sent to them against a Facebook ID. LiveRamp is an ad-tech company that specializes in data services involving identity management and data onboarding for marketing purposes.[81]

"De-identification means removing or modifying personal information so it can no longer be linked to a specific individual. But if you are matching person-specific data against a Facebook ID, then that is identification. When data is used for activation—targeting people who are exposed to an ad and click through to a landing page, and so on—the premise of de-identification falls apart," Garcia emphasizes.

The great ad-tech myth

As third-party cookies were being phased out and privacy awareness rose, the concept of first-party data gained ground. Is first-party data the answer to more sustainable digital advertising?

It depends, Garcia argues. She emphasizes that you first need to realize that it is a myth that more precision is always more effective. If you understand that you do not have to profile and track people at a granular level to succeed with your marketing, you will realize the same thing applies to the data you hold yourself and your direct relationship with leads and customers.

"Sometimes first-party data serves your business and your customers. Especially when brands use it to build a legitimate relationship with their customers, and when publishers use it to build legitimate relationships with their audience. And when brands and publishers with legitimate ambitions come together, things can get really good. Especially, and hopefully, if they can do so without the big platforms getting in the way," she explains and states:

---

[81] Following the interview with Arielle Garcia in December 2023, the organization Open Rights Group filed a group complaint addressing precisely these concerns. Open Rights Group. "ORG submits complaints about intrusive LiveRamp adtech system." Published March 15, 2024: https://www.openrightsgroup.org/press-releases/org-complaint-liveramp-adtech/

"If a company understands its customers better than anyone else, and a publisher offers better content than anyone else, they do not need the precision and tracking to succeed with their marketing."

You cannot keep your cake and eat it too

Unsurprisingly, attempts to replace third-party cookies with other identification solutions like Unified ID and UID 2.0 do not impress Garcia much, because they seem to have the same problems around choice and transparency as cookies.

"I've tried to understand whether they can offer better transparency. So far, I haven't seen that they can," Garcia notes, seeming to indirectly suggest that there is no way to both keep your cake and eat it too. Because the new ID solutions do not solve the dilemma that cookies had, you still need consent here too. At the same time, she is convinced this does not have to be a problem.

"You have to accept that when you are transparent and give people the choice to say yes or no to tracking and profiling, a large portion will say no. You can absolutely create an experience that increases the chances of a 'yes', maybe because the visitor feels they can benefit from it."

Garcia's premise is that we as marketers, media agencies, and publishers need to question old truths and create the market and market conditions that we can stand behind and believe in.

"I hope for, or can envision, a world where publishers band together and offer genuine transparency to consumers, collectively creating better advertising revenue streams. I definitely think there are opportunities here."

"Publishers and advertisers could also tackle the reach problem together, creating real alternatives to the major platforms. Though I'm uncertain whether they'd need a trade desk or platform in the middle to hold that collaboration together."

At the same time, Garcia is concerned about the impact generative AI will have on publishers.

"Time is running short. Change needs to happen before people get accustomed to not clicking through to publishers' sites," she says, referring in part to how Google has rolled out AI-integrated search that answers questions within Google's interface instead of directing users to the websites that created the knowledge. The websites and brands with strong direct search traffic, like major Swedish evening papers, or CNN and Yahoo, will face less pressure from this trend than "everyone else," she says.

At the same time, they are not unaffected.

To illustrate the severity of the situation, she points to how the New York Times and Google struck a $100 million deal over three years that gives the New York Times the right to have its news highlighted on Google.[82]

"If deals like this become the rule rather than the exception, publishers won't just remain dependent on tech giants for advertising revenue, they'll also depend on them for their content to reach audiences. That puts us in a situation where platforms have even greater power over what content gets published," Garcia underlines.

When toddlers click on your ads

One of the uncomfortable truths Garcia highlights is that as an advertiser, you often only see the numbers "they" want you to see. When asked who "they" are, she answers: the intermediaries.

To explain, she references a report from the ANA at the end of 2023, which found that the average advertising campaign

---

[82] *Reuters*. New York Times to get around $100 million from Google over three years, Published May 8, 2023: https://www.reuters.com/business/media-telecom/new-york-times-get-around-100-million-google-over-three-years-wsj-2023-05-08/

was displayed across an average of 44,000 different websites.[83] This is staggering because it indicates that campaigns often have far too broad a reach and low precision, with all that it entails for advertising effectiveness: harder to optimize, higher likelihood of bot clicks, difficulty controlling what potentially questionable sites the ad appears on, and so forth.

"This is how capitalism breaks down in a world where big tech and ad-tech set the rules," Garcia says, continuing:

"Do you understand what a tiny fraction of advertising dollars actually reaches real publishers when the situation looks like this? It is an existence," she says, "that we've arrived at after advertisers were lured away from buying ad placements to buying audiences and impressions."

"They bought into the illusion that you can reach the same target groups by being on thousands more sites and thereby drive down CPM costs.[84] By being on sites where your audience or target group is—which, according to ad-tech platforms' logic, means thousands more websites rather than primarily quality sites with quality content."

"They've conditioned advertisers to fixate on driving down cost per impression, instead of considering whether the results can be validated," she says, telling me about another revealing report produced by Adalytics at the end of 2023.[85]

Adalytics is a company that helps publishers and businesses to understand, among other things, where their advertising dollars go and where their digital ads end up. Few companies want their brand to appear in questionable digital contexts. Adalytics also offers the ability to see how often an ad is shown on a particular website to test, for example, whether the ad-tech

---

[83] Association of National Advertisers (ANA). ANA Programmatic Media Supply Chain Transparency Study: Complete Report. Published December 2023: https://www.ana.net/miccontent/show/id/rr-2023-12-ana-programmatic-media-supply-chain-transparency-study

[84] CPM stands for Cost Per Mille, or cost per thousand impressions.

[85] Adalytics. Are YouTube Ads COPPA Compliant? Published December 2023: https://adalytics.io/blog/are-youtube-ads-coppa-compliant

service—the intermediary—is applying the promised frequency capping that Korzeniowski also mentioned. This is a setting that limits how many times an ad is shown to a particular user during a certain period of time to prevent overexposure and improve user experience.

The report showed that Google-owned YouTube was serving adult-targeted ads to small children. In doing so, they collected personal data from children and shared it with various players in the ad-tech industry, including companies that had been penalized for violating children's privacy rights.

"If we set aside for a moment how problematic this is from a privacy perspective, and instead look at it from a pure marketing perspective: If I am a bank that wants to reach adults with my ads, why are my ads being shown to children?" Garcia asks rhetorically and continues:

"Google tried to wave away the question by saying the children were probably sitting with an adult watching the ads, which I cannot understand for the life of me, since we're talking about cell phone screens, and you see all the children's programs in YouTube's sidebar feed."

"Now add how aggressively Google pushes its AI-driven Performance Max product, which they say is calibrated to show the ads that perform best. But how well does PMax work when it is apparently optimizing your adult ads based on click-through rates from sticky little fingers?"

In other words, advertisers who wonder why PMax does not give them sufficiently granular reports on the contexts where their ads were exposed, may have found their answer here.

"For me, this *Made for Kids* report was an aha moment. It became so clear how everything connects. We have a situation where little children's fingers are clicking on ads, and now the children themselves are being tracked and shown the same ad in other contexts."

"How can ad-tech players continue to claim that you can achieve a balance between the right to privacy and a company's commercial interests, when A) they cannot prove it and B) the situation actually points to the opposite?" Garcia asks and goes on:

"Ad-tech companies like Google want you to believe this balance can be achieved. Their interest is in maintaining the status quo in the ecosystem because it is a profitable business for them. But what about the brands? How do they benefit from this?"

When asked whether the ad-tech industry should be thrown out with the bathwater, she says it depends. She thinks the platforms certainly have value for consumers and that their products could be effective. But the problem, she says, is that they have had too much free rein for too long, leading to blind profit maximization.

"They've been unregulated and unable to regulate themselves. Profit comes before everything, even before their customers' businesses. That is why I think the business model for data brokers driven by third-party data is fundamentally on its last legs."

She also hopes it will not be able to save itself.

"They'll certainly try everything they can. I see, for example, how some players are trying to move their data aggregation operations to the first-party side. They'll create vague contracts to access customers' first-party data that they'll claim is 'de-identified' according to their homemade definition of this."

"But for firms that work purely with third-party data—for example, those who buy third-party data from other sources, or those with their own SDKs that they collect data with, or even better, those who buy data from other firms with SDKs to avoid responsibility, they're beyond saving," Garcia says, as she continues:

"Right now, however, I have bigger political issues in my sight. We know that government agencies also buy data from these data brokers. I also think they'll become more creative about how they can get closer to lawmakers and regulatory authorities."

But Garcia thinks there could be room for intermediaries, for example those that connect supply and demand sides without having a built-in dependence on consumer data.

"They just need to be better regulated and verified in a credible way. Some business models in this ecosystem are more challenging than others," she thinks.

Marketers use bad data to target fake people on unsafe websites

After Garcia left UM Worldwide, she started her own consulting firm, ASG Solution. But fairly soon (after our interview), Garcia was recruited by the nonprofit Check My Ads Institute, where she now serves as the Chief Operating Officer. It is a role that fits her like a glove, since Check My Ads' mission is to scrutinize and reform the digital advertising industry, which, as they emphasize, is absolutely necessary if there is to be a sustainable future for democracy.

Garcia returns to how the ad-tech ecosystem is "complexity by design," stressing that marketers have been caught between agencies and the major platforms. Her hypothesis is that if you succeed in educating and empowering marketers so they know what questions to ask, then they and their agencies can hold platforms accountable. If they do not, it is the marketer and agency who get blamed and bear full responsibility.

Let us go back to the example of ads intended for adults that were shown to children.

"If, you as a marketer and agency, are confronted by a client, can you prove to the client that her ads were not exposed to children? If you cannot, it is because the platform you use to place ads cannot provide you with the required transparency", she explains and goes on.

"Situations like this create useful friction between the agency and the platforms, forcing the agency to stop accepting the platforms' excuses and start making demands instead."

Garcia stresses that there are so many problematic myths around ad-tech, myths that maintain a system "where marketers continue using bad data to reach fictional people on unsafe websites." She believes that by examining these myths, you can get to the heart of the problem.

Why have marketers not pushed back in any significant way already?

Garcia thinks that one factor slowing down change is that marketers are afraid of losing their jobs. The platforms make it easy for marketers to access the ROI figures they want them to focus on. As a marketer, you know what you have, but not what you could get, because what is the alternative when the platforms are so big and all-encompassing?

"But," Garcia says, "when you start examining what variables the ROI figures are based on, what value they're measuring. you can begin to question whether the payoff is the most advantageous for you and your client. You can stop fixating on having the lowest possible CPM costs," she says and continus:

"You can start debunking the myth you are living in and hopefully come to the conclusion that prioritizing ad buys in quality publications is ultimately not a more costly affair at all."

She explains that if you decide to focus your advertising only on a list of quality publications, advertising costs will be higher than if you let each ad campaign appear on "an average of 44,000 websites"—i.e., often everywhere instead of in the right contexts online, as the ANA report showed.

"But the follow-up questions you then need to ask yourself," she says, "are around how much you are spending on licenses for third-party data, or so-called data clean rooms, or fees to the agency, and the entire ad-tech complex that acts as intermediary."

"What would happen if you said 'no, I'm not running any programmatic at all this year'? What would happen if you tried that?"

"I'm not naive," Garcia adds.

She does not think marketers will flock quickly to a new paradigm. But she does believe in the power that materializes when myths are shattered, that it is possible to create a roadmap that is tempting enough for the marketer and their short-term metrics.

"They need to be convinced that it can be worth testing, and that there is value at the end of the period that doesn't just mean more expensive CPM costs, so they do not see it as a threat to their livelihood."

"As a marketer, you do not need to know everything about a lead to reach them. You need to ask yourself what potential customers expect from the brand at different stages of their relationship with the brand. Sometimes retargeting might be a good idea; other times it might be better to appear in a particular context where the customer is likely to be."

Garcia wants people to broaden their thinking and stop focusing on what technical solutions and signals should replace, for example, the third-party cookie, and instead focus on how to create long-term sustainable relationships with customers and leads.

"The gold standard for me would be if agencies, as a result of client demands, confronted the platforms and said they won't pay until they get detailed placement reports on all products and placements, plus the ability for truly independent third-party verification and measurement. Plus full transparency into how the targeting of products works, especially those driven by algorithms."

"Such transparency requirements wouldn't be derived from a privacy perspective, but it would serve that cause and create a possible domino effect, because we cannot achieve any change without transparency."

When asked if change is possible, Garcia answers that we have now reached a kind of ground zero, that awareness and debate have become more vocal and grow stronger.

"People today distrust advertising and advertisers, companies cannot trust that their advertising and media agencies are protecting their interests, and no one trusts the big tech platforms. How sustainable is that? It is becoming increasingly difficult for the industry to convince itself that people think it is okay for their personal data to be taken without informed consent in exchange for advertising that is marginally more relevant at best."

And she does not feel alone in her calling and her work. The tide is turning.

"I'm optimistic," she says.

15. The bombers & the blind spot

During World War II, British researchers analyzed damage on returning bombers to determine where the planes needed reinforcement. Which parts of the aircrafts took the most hits? By identifying these areas, they could armor existing planes and build new aircrafts with reinforcement in the "right places."

Enter statistician Abraham Wald.

He scratched his head and wondered, "Hold on—what about the bombers that never came back?"

The planes that did not return, had likely been fatally hit precisely where the returning planes showed no damage. At which point everyone probably went, "Oh right, we did not think of that."

Wald pointed out that the researchers had fallen victim to what is called survivorship bias.

The story of the bombers illustrates just how easy it is to reach false conclusions when you are working from flawed assumptions or asking the wrong questions of your data. Today, in our hyper-data-driven marketing landscape, we are facing a situation where you as an advertiser (and media buyer) can be systematically deceived. This makes recognizing survivorship bias both more critical and more challenging. How can we accurately measure success when we cannot trust the underlying data?

Let me give you an example. In late March 2024, Adalytics—the company Garcia referenced—released yet another study[86] that erodes trust and illustrates how as an advertiser "you do not know what you do not know," so to

---

[86] *Adalytics*. Ads Observed on www3.Forbes Subdomain. Published December 2023, updated April 2, 2024. https://adalytics.io/blog/ads-observed-on-www3-forbes-subdomain#conclusion

speak. This time it concerns the way in which the global media platform Forbes[87] had misled its advertisers.

Instead of getting ad space on the forbes.com domain, major advertisers and brands had purchased and received exposure on www3.forbes.com, i.e., a substandard subdomain with lower content quality that Forbes had been using since at least 2017.

On this subdomain, readers were exposed to significantly more ads compared to those who landed on the main domain, and the content was not even indexed by search engines: While a reader on "real" Forbes might see 3-10 ads per article, a reader on the junk site received over 201 impressions per session/page visit.

And where did the visitors come from?

Forbes funneled 70 percent of visitors through content recommendation platforms like Taboola and Outbrain. In other words, they were buying the traffic. Adalytics was also able to document that the largest age group on the fake domain was 55–64 years old, not the 25–34 range found on the real domain.

Furthermore, on the real domain, 90 percent of the visitors arrive through organic searches and direct searches. The mismatch between where advertisers expected their ads to appear versus where they were actually exposed, was in other words diametrically opposed.

Was it just a crime of opportunity?

As Garcia points out, there are economic incentives for a publisher like Forbes to cheat, since you as a publisher gain a larger profit the more people see and/or click on the ad. In the Forbes case, it is about impressions. They gain their profit from ad impressions, which is measured as cost per thousand—Cost Per Mille (CPM). In the study, they also documented how one

---

[87] *The Drum.* Forbes accused of selling MFA media to brands under guise of legitimate ad space. Published April 4, 2024:
https://www.thedrum.com/news/2024/04/04/forbes-accused-selling-mfa-media-brands-under-guise-legitimate-ad-space

advertiser paid a CPM of $60 for one (1!) specific visit. The advertiser was the New York Times. And Forbes managed this feat by exposing the specific visitor to 27 subscription ads on a single occasion, which happened while the person was looking at a slideshow about "the fifty richest people in the world."

As soon as the story broke, Forbes removed the subdomain faster than you could say "scandal."

That Forbes could not resist the temptation to deceive its advertisers, does not (necessarily) mean that the lightning-fast real-time processes for targeted ad buying should be scrapped entirely. The point, as Garcia highlights, is perhaps rather that neither the buyers, intermediaries, nor sellers in the ad-tech market should assume that brands will buy blind and trust that all players in the technically complicated selling and buying chain have honorable intentions. An advertiser like the New York Times should have asked what Forbes was measuring and whether it could be defined as success. This obviously requires that Forbes operate transparently and can prove they are telling the truth. And it is this lack of transparency, combined with the complexity by design in the ad-tech systems that creates the opportunity for fraud.

At the same time, one needs to keep in mind that in the foreground of this story are, as Korzeniowski pointed out, the $783.46 billion per year that the global ad-tech industry turns over. And, not least, its most dominant player, Google's parent company Alphabet, derives 80-85 percent[88] of its total earnings from digital advertising.

---

[88] Percentage: Approximately 80-85% of Alphabet's total revenue derives from digital advertising. This includes revenue from Google Ads (search advertising), YouTube ads, and display advertising via Google Display Network.

Company	Market Share (%)	Annual Revenue Billions USD
Alphabet	30	147
Meta	25	84
Amazon	12	31
Microsoft	4	8
Verizon Media	3	2.5
X (Twitter)	2	1.7
Snapchat	1	1
All Others	23	N/A

Source: Statista 2024

In other words, the online advertising market is an oligopoly. But when these monopolistic companies face criticism, they are quick to claim that "we're the biggest because we're the best" and even paint themselves as the heroes of the story since their solutions are both necessary and ideal for small and medium-sized businesses. But does it hold water?

Mark with the sign

"Say you have a pedestrian street in Oslo with a bunch of different shops," says Erik Bugge, as he continues.

"On this street, there is also a guy walking around named Mark. Mark carries different advertising signs. One day, Mark walks into one of the shops and asks the business owner if she could not tell him everything about her customers. Mark wants to know absolutely everything. What they buy, what they like, who they might interact with, and so on."

Mark thinks more is more.

"Now here's the thing," Bugge continues, "Mark has one condition for the shop, and that is that he gets to use whatever data the shop shares with him for absolutely anything he wants."

"The shop owner says OK to the deal, and Mark thanks her and heads out onto the pedestrian street. After a while, he spots a customer walking toward a café."

The customer, Bugge explains, likes cortados. Mark knows this because he has plenty of cafés feeding him information about this particular customer. Mark also has advertising contracts with every café on the street. And the one that pays him the most happens to be around the corner. So Mark quickly holds up a sign offering half-price cortados at—you guessed it—the café around the corner. The customer sees this and decides to head there instead, which means Mark pockets the biggest commission since the place pays him the most money for every conversion his sign generates.

The man telling this story is Erik Bugge, founder and CEO of Kobler, an advertising platform that reaches target audiences based on the content of a page or article. And it runs completely without personal data or tracking. It is called contextual marketing.

Bugge is an engineer who founded his company when he studied in Trondheim. But it did not start out as an advertising platform. Instead, he had developed a search engine service for individual domains. Their first major client was Norway's parliament.

Bugge and his team hoped to scale the business to the Swedish parliament and other institutions of similar stature, but they quickly realized that few organizations had pockets as deep as the Norwegian government. As a result, they began brainstorming what else they could do with their platform.

The lightbulb moment came when they stumbled upon something interesting: If they placed an ad with messaging that aligned with the text or content of the search results, it delivered massive results for the advertiser.

This was about twelve years ago.

The first version of the contextual platform was pitched to publishers like Schibsted and Aller Media. But the business model hit a wall and proved hard to scale. Not because the platform itself could not deliver—it was built to serve ads across multiple news sites and publications simultaneously. The "problem" lay on the supply side, with the publishers themselves, since each publisher sold their own ad inventory directly to advertisers.

If the demand side—the advertisers—wanted to cast a wide net, they would have to reach out and negotiate separate deals with every single publication, even though Kobler could handle ad placement across all sites and in the right contexts. Kobler could connect all the dots seamlessly, but advertisers and publishers still had to hammer out the contract details themselves.

To give you an example: If a company wanted to advertise their new electric bikes and reach environmentally conscious readers, they would need to cut individual deals with *Dagens Nyheter*, *Expressen*, *Svenska Dagbladet*, and so on. Needless to say, this made the whole process cumbersome and time-consuming for advertisers, especially when running larger campaigns. To solve this problem, they decided to transform it into a self-service platform that targeted advertisers directly.

Anyone who has worked in logistics and transport administration will find this familiar, since it mirrors how modern freight booking platforms operate. But instead of advertisers and publishers, you have companies that need to ship goods (equivalent to the advertiser) and transport companies that can haul the freight (equivalent to the publishers). The target audience for such a platform is the companies that need to move goods around, not the freight companies themselves. The relationship with the freight companies is built around integrating them technically into the platform, since each freight company typically has its own technical languages and systems.

Just a side note, Kobler means connecting in Norwegian.

I find this incredibly illuminating for understanding how the web functions as a marketplace, and the technical challenges that can arise in the absence of sustainable standards—and solid industry collaboration. Imagine if publishers had understood early on the dangers posed by middlemen like Google and Meta (Facebook) and acted to build solutions that protected their own existence and, by extension, their vital journalistic mission.

Nevertheless, the new platform was developed alongside several Norwegian media agencies and launched in 2019—the year after the GDPR went into full effect—which boosted Bugge's and his colleagues' confidence. They figured "this is going to change everything," which was also one of the reasons the platform was tracking-free by design.

Bugge does not mince words when he says that the GDPR is fundamentally incompatible with the kind of advertising that tracks and profiles people using third-party data.

He points to how sluggishly data protection authorities have conducted their oversight, and how they often seem to misunderstand their own mandate. This probably stems from either not daring, or not bothering, to examine how retargeting actually works, both technically and commercially, which allows a giant like Mark Zuckerberg's Facebook to remain the elephant in the room that nobody talks about.

Because a business model like Facebook is basically Zuckerberg on the walkabout, but on steroids.

And, holding the pen here, I can relate to the reluctance to engage, as you know. But now that I know more than I sometimes wish I did, I have to sign off on what Bugge is trying to convey when he describes the situation as absolutely bonkers.

"That companies tell Mark on the street everything about their customers and agree to let Mark use that data however serves him best is insanity. But they do it because they've lost all perspective, I think. And because it is so convenient to just install a pixel and hit play. But this is not marketing. It is a pyramid scheme," Bugge says, and explains.

"If you do not agree to Mark's terms, your competitors will use the data to their advantage at your expense. Meanwhile, you'll be forced to pay more and more just to maintain your position in the market."

"When Meta says, 'we're so great for small businesses,' I'd argue it is exactly the opposite. Small and medium-sized businesses are like cash cows for Facebook," Bugge continues.

Throughout our conversation, he keeps putting his finger at how dysfunctional a marketplace becomes under monopoly-like conditions. How commerce ultimately becomes unsustainable if no one is playing by the same rules.

"I often draw parallels to environmental pollution. Let us say factories are required not to dump dirty water into a river. The companies that spend money following the law in this area become losers if regulatory authorities do not punish those who break the law. It is the same thing with the GDPR. If authorities do not enforce their oversight requirements, the status quo continues."

At the same time, Bugge understands that many regulatory authorities might be reluctant to engage, since taking on a process against companies like Meta or Google is not easy. They refuse transparency to the bitter end and have unlimited financial resources. That is why he sympathizes with the decision to develop two regulations that address this dilemma in different ways—the Digital Markets Act (DMA) and the Digital Services Act (DSA).

Bugge, who sits on one of the working groups for online advertising in the European Commission, was asked during the DSA legislative process to provide expert testimony to the European Parliament. In his submission (the recording can be found online) he advocates for an outright ban on retargeting based on third-party data, arguing it would protect small and medium-sized businesses while creating incentives for sustainable innovation in the digital advertising market.

In his speech, he specifically calls out a number of lobby groups that had also been given a platform and claimed to represent small businesses—but were actually bought and paid for, since their membership base could not be verified. This phenomenon is called astroturfing,[89] he explains, and it is a method where oligopolies/monopolies like Google and Meta create or support organizations that appear to represent small and medium-sized businesses, but in reality, these organizations are driven by the agenda of the big companies. The goal is to make it look like their views and interests are supported by ordinary small businesses, even though they are not.

The ban on retargeting based on third-party data did not make it into the DSA, despite having a majority in the parliament. Bugge says he is not surprised, since "DSA was the most lobbied legislation ever."

"But I'm of the opinion that the GDPR is sufficient to practically eliminate this type of invasive advertising, provided that regulatory authorities ensure the law is followed."

The GDPR through proxy

At the same time, progress towards a more sustainable advertising market online, does not entirely depend on regulatory authorities' independence and drive. Even for Bugge and Kobler, the story of third-party cookie phase-out has been a force to reckon with. Bugge goes so far as to say that Safari and Firefox, with their privacy protocols (ITP and ETP respectively), have effectively implemented the GDPR through proxy.

"We've worked with privacy engineers at Apple and followed the development of ITP. And in 2020, when they introduced version 14.5, we saw that from a certain point

---

[89] Stolton, Samuel. Big tech Astroturfing: Who Speaks for Small EU Companies, Eyes on Washington? *Politico EU Influence Newsletter*, March 15, 2023: https://www.politico.eu/newsletter/politico-eu-influence/big-tech-astroturfing-who-speaks-for-small-eu-companies-eyes-on-washington-2/

forward, you could no longer follow a consumer across websites and ad streams."

This was something Kobler leveraged in their own marketing, since Apple—and thus Safari—has a strong market share among affluent users in the Nordics. And companies that realized they could no longer reach these users the same way felt compelled to rethink their advertising budgets.

A similar effect comes from stricter requirements from the EDPB and the regulatory authorities of various countries regarding how cookie banners must be designed. When Denmark pointed the finger squarely at the issue and said there must be a "yes" button and a "no" button on the first layer of the banner, the percentage of people who said "reject all" jumped from 15 to 30 percent, he says.

"Combine these two variables and access to your target audience drops significantly in the programmatic system," Bugge points out.

When asked whether Kobler's customer base is particularly concerned about data protection and the GDPR, Bugge answers, "No, not really."

"Even though privacy is part of our brand, we do not sell on that. We emphasize that it is a more effective type of advertising because you reach your entire target audience. So while regulatory decisions and technical restrictions help increase interest in Kobler, it is the results the platform generates that create loyalty and customer satisfaction," Bugge argues.

"Some of our biggest customers give us practically unlimited budgets."

Kobler is, as Bugge puts it, "not a utopia where you install a pixel on your website and hit play." They completely reject the reasoning that "more personal data equals better advertising," and say, "Hey, it is actually not such a dumb idea to place an ad for cat food in a pet magazine, next to an article about the importance of diet to cat health, instead of in a car publication next to an article about fourth-generation carburetors."

With full focus on context and relevance, you also never risk ending up on some junk page on a mysterious Forbes subdomain with questionable content.

I do not find it hard to understand why Kobler has grown steadily over the years and is expanding to multiple markets, regulatory sluggishness notwithstanding. Name a brand that does not feel flattered by instantly landing in the right context. That is something entirely different from stalking your customers with an ad for those red tennis shoes they bought last week on Zalando.

Bugge also explains how the platform takes you back to the fundamentals of how successful marketing worked before the surveillance bonanza. And it appeals to creatives because instead of paying with your customers' personal data in pursuit of direct-response metrics, you get to focus more on your creative ability to reach your target audience based on your understanding of and feel for the people behind the consumers—the psychology and what your product has to offer.

"It is a more creative approach, but through an advanced technical tool that you can also use for immediate tactical moves, like newsjacking," he says.

Stats on their terms

If as Bugge claims, Kobler's contextual solution positively surprises advertisers, what does that say about its opposite— retargeting based on surveillance and Mark's sign on the pedestrian street? An undeniable contrast emerges between them. While Kobler seems to work because the advertiser's sales figures speak for themselves (in the advertisers' own business systems), reports about low data reliability from "the others" keep piling up.

Bugge thinks we should look at what researchers Michael Braun, Bart de Langhe, Stefano Puntoni, and Eric M. Schwartz have demonstrated: that Meta misleads both small and large companies about how effective their advertising actually is on the platform.[90]

On one hand, Meta offers businesses tools and advice for succeeding with their advertising and improving results. On the other hand, they do not provide an accurate picture of the real impact of advertising. The researchers are particularly critical of how Facebook conducts its so-called A/B testing.

A fundamental principle of A/B testing is randomly dividing your target audience into two groups, each of which sees its own version of an ad. But Facebook instead uses machine learning that optimizes ad delivery based on user data. This means certain groups—younger people, for example—might see a particular ad more often than others. Because of this, the groups seeing different ads are no longer comparable, since they differ in more ways than just which ad they have seen. This leads to misleading results about the effectiveness of the ads. At least in the long term.

Facebook optimizes ad delivery on user data in this way to deliver higher click-through rates and better short-term results, so advertisers can see an immediate bump in clicks and engagement since the ads are shown to users Facebook knows are most likely to interact with them. But as an advertiser, you cannot conclude that one ad is better than another, because unknown factors have influenced the results.

The researchers shine a spotlight on the fact that the platform does not help you to understand what actually causes a click or conversion—what the real cause-and-effect relationship is, the causality. Instead, they work with predictions or forecasts that can mislead advertisers about the true effectiveness of their campaigns.

Other researchers, in line with Braun, Langhe, Puntoni and Schwartz, have highlighted how the major platforms from

[90] Braun, Michael, Bart de Langhe, Stefano Puntoni, and Eric M. Schwartz,"Leveraging Digital Advertising Platforms for Consumer Research." *Journal of Consumer Research* 51 (1): 119–128. Published 2024. https://doi.org/10.1093/jcr/ucad058.

Google and Meta also love to claim their ads have driven higher sales than they have by over-attributing conversions and sales, i.e., taking credit for conversions that happened for other reasons, like direct sales or organic traffic.

Journalist James Hercher from AdExchanger is one such voice. He reports, for example, how the numbers that platforms deliver, do not always align with advertisers' own figures in their order and customer management systems (CRM). [91]

A timber wholesaler, for instance, describes situations where their salespeople have been in direct contact with a company, had multiple calls and email conversations, and where their dedicated website is not integrated with Google or Meta in any way. Yet they still see how the platforms attribute results to themselves.

The timber wholesaler in question says he has no idea how they pull off this trick, but that he is fascinated, almost impressed. Hercher also explains that a similar situation exists in the mobile app market and among food industry brands. Since he is referring to the American market, he does not only mention Google, Meta, and Amazon, but also Walmart, Target, Kroger, and many smaller retail networks. They often attribute conversions to themselves everywhere, and it can happen without any connection to the seasonal or monthly sales results of the brand, Hercher claims. This means that even if sales always drop in April for a certain brand or increase right before Valentine's Day, the reports from the platforms still show a constant increase due to ad results.

It is as if advertisers are being spoon-fed survivor bias. And when we zoom out, we are reminded that what we are seeing up close are symptoms of a skewed advertising market suffering from oligopoly.

---

[91] Broussard, Zach. "Walled Garden Platforms Are Drowning Marketers in Self-Attributed Sales," *AdExchanger*, April 17, 2024:
https://www.adexchanger.com/commerce/walled-garden-platforms-are-drowning-marketers-in-self-attributed-sales/

Facebook, for example, is the world's largest social media platform, with over 3 billion daily users. It is easy to understand why companies want to be there. Or why it is nearly impossible not to engage with the platform. But if you as a company do not know how Facebook's algorithm works, or what "Mark" does with all the personal data you share with "him," how can you ever protect and guarantee your customers' privacy? Or your own business integrity and relationship with your customers? And not least—how do you know that the budget you spend there gives you more bang for your buck than if you had not spent it there?

Bugge himself thinks the situation becomes even stranger when publishers and website owners, instead of getting to the bottom of the fundamental problem and addressing how they can earn the market's trust, pin their hopes on cookie banners and the expectation that such a high percentage of visitors will just reflexively say yes to sometimes hundreds of different tracking cookies. Or "informationskapslar" as they are called in Norwegian.

The inconvenient truth

Neither Bugge, Pols, Garci, Korzeniowski, nor those behind studies on issues like over-attribution claim that retargeting based on third-party data does not always work. Rather, they seem to question how this became the only answer, why companies went along with it blindly, and how it can continue to grow despite the lack of compliance, and despite the problems piling up in its wake seeming to be features, not bugs.

It has been thirty years since the Netscape cookie was hacked so that companies and marketers could claim the right to monitor, track, and profile individuals without talking about it openly. This was a development that grew in intensity when we wandered into the platform-based web we now call Web 2.0, where we have gotten used to concepts like pixels, super cookies, fingerprinting, and a marketplace dominated by Google, Meta, and Amazon.

This web is now in a process aimed at holding its most influential players accountable in a way that the GDPR, despite its mandate, has so far failed to achieve: Even though some teeth have been filed down, the powerful EU regulations Digital Markets Act and Digital Services Act—under the motto "What is illegal offline must be illegal online"—have already forced Google to require that everyone using GA4 and Google Ads does not do so without obtaining proper consent from their respective visitors and users. Not to mention Safari's and Firefox's "GDPR through proxy," as Bugge put it.

In the US, it is no longer only California that has a privacy regulation. As of this writing, there are five U.S. states with their own GDPR, and another ten are on track to get one. Meanwhile, there is a bipartisan proposition at the federal level that at least gets an "A for effort."

We are thus at a crucial crossroads with an opportunity to soul-search and regroup. But what does it mean for the digital marketer and advertiser?

The facts suggest that granular profiling and tracking of people online costs more than it is worth. But it is an uncomfortable truth. It is also an uncomfortable truth that we are locked into a market dominated by oligopoly.

But if you have read this far, you are probably ready to embrace uncomfortable truths, not least the latter, since "capitalism without competition is not capitalism, it is exploitation," as President Joe Biden put it.[92]

With that motto in mind, let me roll out the red carpet for the final section of my book with a story about one of the world's most successful companies and brands, and the decisions that led to its decline over the past four years. I think this story puts

---

[92] Feuer, Will. "Biden signs executive order aimed at limiting anticompetitive practices," *CBS News*, July 9, 2021: https://www.cbsnews.com/news/biden-executive-order-anticompetitive-economic-practices-watch-live-stream-today-2021-07-09/

the last 25 years of web development as a marketplace into perspective.

Not all decision-makers understand the value of people who can spot survivor bias and shout "that is a correlation, not causation."

16. To fix what is not broken

Lessons from Nike's pivot.

In our age of ChatGPT and algorithmic everything, we are constantly told that data and AI can replace human intuition. That creativity can be automated. That machines soon will understand what moves people better than people themselves can. This machine-first thinking, is not a new story. And in one way, Nike's $70 billion fall offers the perfect cautionary tale of what happens when this allure-in-the-machine-thinking takes hold.

Let us go back to the beginning.

On June 28, 2024, Nike lost $25 billion in market value. In a single day. It was the culmination of a nine-month decline that had wiped out a total of $70 billion from the company's value. On this day, the stock fell to its lowest level since 2018, and trading volume—the number of Nike shares bought and sold—skyrocketed to thirteen times normal levels. In other words, it was a unpleasant day for Nike on Wall Street.

In a viral LinkedIn article from the summer of 2024, the former brand strategist for Nike, Massimo Giunco dissects what went wrong.[93] Giunco calls it the story of a self-inflicted collapse, and it is a deeply revealing reporting. A tale that begins on January 13, 2020, when John Donahoe takes over as CEO from Mark Parker.

Together with Heidi O'Neill, who gets the title President of Consumer, Product & Brand, Donahoe pivots the Nike ship 180 degrees toward ... well, down. Giunco describes how, after a quick tour of the company he had been asked to lead, the new CEO sends out an email to all employees. He opens the email with "Dear Nike colleagues, this is what you asked for ..." and

---

[93] Giunco, Massimo. "Nike: An Epic Saga of Value Destruction," *LinkedIn*, July 28, 2024: https://www.linkedin.com/pulse/nike-epic-saga-value-destruction-massimo-giunco-llplf/

then presents three decisions aimed at fundamentally transforming the company.

First, Donahoe says, Nike will eliminate all product categories from the organization—across brand, product development, and sales. Second, Nike will become a direct-to-consumer company and wave goodbye to the wholesale tier. And third, Nike will centralize its marketing and make it data-driven—digitally data-driven.

What Nike was before the algorithm

For fifty years, Nike had built one of the world's most powerful brands on a deceptively simple foundation: They understood the power of archetypical storytelling, which people can relate to. They chose the story of the fighter, and the theme of everyday people achieving extraordinary things.

This understanding was not abstract. It was embedded in how Nike organized itself. The company built deep expertise around specific sports—running, basketball, soccer, fitness—with specialists who did not just know the technical requirements of each discipline, but understood the psychology, culture, and emotional landscape of each sport. And you could see it play out in campaigns like "Human Race", where Nike during the Beijing Olympics in 2008 got the whole world running from Los Angeles to Rio, from Rome to Seoul, From Tokyo to Istanbul, from Paris to London. And so the "Just Do It" brand was reinvented repeatedly. This was the Nike that Donahoe inherited in 2020—a brand built on understanding what moves people at the deepest level.

Fixing things that were not broken

When Donahoe announced his three decisions, the company that had mastered the art of understanding what moves people to action, and product off the shelves, began to systematically dismantle that capability.

The first change eliminated product categories meant destroying the deep sports expertise that had been Nike's competitive advantage. According to Giunco, this came on McKinsey's recommendation. The consulting giant argued that Nike's specialist structure led to duplicate work, and that a "data-driven insight model" could replace knowledge-based product development. Instead of experts who understood the unique psychology of runners versus basketball players, Nike reorganized around demographics: men's, women's, kids'. They became a clothing retailer optimized by data rather than a sports company guided by human understanding.

Next, the direct-to-consumer pivot replaced decades of retailer relationships and market knowledge with e-commerce optimization. As Giunco describes it, wholesale would be downgraded to secondary status while Nike Direct—led by Nike.com—would become the primary revenue source. The algorithm would determine demand better than the retailers who had been selling Nike products to real customers for decades.

Third, Data-driven marketing replaced Nike's legendary storytelling with what Giunco calls "content production for digital channels." Instead of breakthrough campaigns that moved culture, Nike would create thousands of small, optimized pieces designed to drive traffic to Nike.com. Creative human insight about what inspires people would be subordinated to what the data said would generate clicks.

Each decision seemed to represent the same bet: that algorithmic systems could not just supplement human judgment but replace it entirely.

Losing touch with reality

The results did not take long to materialize, and they were spectacular in all the wrong ways.

The inventory nightmare became legendary. Giunco documents how Nike's stock levels spiraled from $6.5 billion in May 2021 to $8.5 billion in May 2022, finally hitting $10 billion by November 2022. The "data-driven flywheel" that was supposed to predict demand better than human expertise had left Nike drowning in products they could not sell. The company that had once mastered the art of creating demand by generating desire could no longer figure out what people actually wanted to buy.

The customer exodus was equally dramatic. When Nike cut ties with longtime retail partners to focus on direct sales, something unexpected happened: customers did not follow them online. As Giunco puts it, Nike had underestimated a fundamental truth—consumers are neither as adaptable nor as loyal as corporate leaders hope. When casual customers could not find Nike shoes in "their" stores, they simply chose other brands. The data models had missed something basic about human behavior: People shop where it is convenient, not where brands want them to shop.

Inevitably the pricing collapse followed. Nike.com became a permanent sale site. Black Friday stretched into Black November, then merged with post-Christmas sales and New Year promotions. What had been premium products commanding premium prices became heavily discounted commodities. Profit margins fell from 46 cents per dollar to 43.5 cents—a devastating blow for a company of Nike's size.

Meanwhile, the creative destruction was equally telling. Giunco contrasts Nike's 2008 "Human Race" campaign—which got the whole world running—with their 2024 Olympic effort: "Defy the Distance: Nike Running Challenge," where consumers could win 20 percent off if they ran 5 kilometers. The company had gone from moving culture to offering coupons.

Should all programmatic be off the table?

The story of Nike's dramatic decline under CEO John Donahoe illustrates many of the themes we have explored: the false promises of surveillance-based advertising, the limitations of programmatic systems, and the danger of prioritizing metrics over meaning.

Brand strategist Giunco's viral analysis of Nike's self-inflicted collapse reveals how a company built on human creativity and authentic storytelling systematically dismantled everything that made it great in favor of a "data-driven flywheel." The result was not optimization—it was destruction.

Does it mean that all programmatic advertising should be off the table? Not if it is privacy-compliant and transparent—as companies like Kobler demonstrate. But the lesson is not that every performance-driven agency is failing their clients. Sophisticated agencies successfully blend creative storytelling with programmatic buying, delivering impressive ROI while building genuine brand value. Long-term brand strategy and short-term programmatic tactics can dance together. The surveillance-based advertising industry generates hundreds of billions for a reason. Well, at least for its service providers.

The real issue is not whether surveillance-based advertising can generate returns today. It is whether businesses can afford to build their future on practices that treat customers as data points rather than human beings, especially as privacy regulations tighten, democratic discourse erodes, and consumer trust dies.

We used to say that personal data was the new oil. But like fossil fuels, surveillance-based advertising pollutes the environment it operates in—corrupting decision-making, eroding trust, and ultimately making the digital marketplace a less healthy place for everyone. Running marketing on this kind of extractive fuel is unsustainable.

For me, what stands out most from the Nike story is how the company lost touch with who they were and what they stood for. This was a company that put their money where their values were—sponsoring quarterback Colin Kaepernick in 2018 when he was blacklisted by the NFL for kneeling during the national anthem to protest police brutality. Nike's "Believe in something. Even if it means sacrificing everything" campaign was financially risky but showed they understood that authentic brand building sometimes requires taking a stand. And they believed in long-term relationships with retailers and were in it for the long haul.

And then what happened?

The market eventually forced a reckoning. In September 2024, Nike announced that John Donahoe would retire, and Elliott Hill—a 30-year Nike veteran who had been head of global consumer and marketing operations before retiring in 2020—would return as CEO. Hill represents what Nike had lost, and his first moves signaled a return to Nike's core: to focus on innovation in running and basketball, to limit availability of overexposed classics like Air Force 1 to restore their mystique, and to reduce dramatically dependence on programmatic advertising in favor of creative brand-building. He is putting the athlete and sport back at the center of the brand.

The market responded positively—Nike stock rose 8-9 percent after Hill's appointment—but as Giunco predicted, the road back will neither be quick nor cheap. It will take years to rebuild the lost expertise in product development, to repair damaged retailer relationships, and to restore the cultural relevance of the brand. You cannot just flip a switch and recover decades of accumulated human insight.

Nike's story is not over. But it serves as a powerful reminder that if something seems too good to be true, it probably is too good to be true. That in our rush toward algorithmic solutions, and fast results, we risk losing the irreplaceable human elements that not only drive business success but should indeed drive it. Some things—understanding what moves people, building authentic relationships, creating meaning that transcends transactions—simply require the distinctly human capabilities that no amount of data can, nor should, replace.

It is not nostalgia. It is merely good business.

V

The Privacy Balance

17. Privacy first marketing

How do you master privacy as a marketer?

Following the chapters about data protection regulations, the web as a dysfunctional marketplace, the paralyzing grip of oligopolies, and the ambivalence of supervisory authorities, you might feel a migraine coming on. But let me head that off at the pass with a glass of water and some aspirin by pointing out that things do not have to be so damn complicated, especially not if you are already a seasoned marketer who has dealt with just about everything in an industry that runs on tight deadlines and impossible KPIs.

Picture this: You have two bars on an x-axis. One is labeled "GDPR/Data Protection Regulations," the other "Ad-Tech." The y-axis measures complexity levels—the taller the bar, the more complex it is. I promise you, the ad-tech bar towers like a skyscraper next to the modest townhouse that is the GDPR. Compared to the technical ecosystem the ad-tech industry has built, the General Data Protection Regulation is almost elegant in its clarity. The problem is that we often get lost in the weeds and miss the fundamental principles—the whole point of the legislation. To make this more manageable, I am going to present a framework that has helped me navigate the privacy jungle. It is a framework I have developed to make it easier for others who want to find their way to a more compliant situation from a data protection perspective.

Two circles & a ground for consent

To get a clear handle on what lawmakers want us to do, let us start by drawing a simple Venn diagram with two overlapping circles. The left circle represents the GDPR, the right represents the ePrivacy Directive. Where the circles overlap, we find consent.

As we have established, the GDPR defines what valid consent is—one of six possible lawful bases for processing personal data. Meanwhile, the ePrivacy Directive says you must have consent before placing cookies on a visitor's browser or tracking them across the web. But while the GDPR deals with the right to privacy and personal integrity, ePrivacy primarily protects the right to confidential communication, i.e., that is, the right to think and communicate freely without being eavesdropped on or tracked.

Why is this important to understand as a marketer?

Well, it puts a finger on what this is really about: respect for the individual. And if you grasp this fundamental point—that we are dealing with a basic human right—it becomes easier to navigate the technical implementation of these principles.

Now, companies or brands and their marketing departments can have different levels of ambition in this area. However, before we dive into that, we first need to clarify two other central concepts from the GDPR that complement the consent principle, concepts you should always keep in your back pocket alongside consent. Namely, data minimization and purpose limitation.

Less is more

Data minimization is exactly what it sounds like: Do not collect more data than you need. It might seem obvious, but in the digital economy it has become standard practice to hoover up as much data as possible, believing it is always good to have. Think about your own experience. How many times have you filled out a contact form asking for your birthday, phone number, and mailing address—when all you wanted was to download a report? What does the company need all that information for?

This is where purpose limitation comes into play. For every data point you want to collect, you must justify why you need it and what you will use it for. And here you need to be specific. "We might want to call you later" is not a valid reason to ask for a phone number. "We'll call you within 24 hours to schedule a meeting"—now that is a different story. And you must think through your purposes before you throw up a form or send data to a third party.

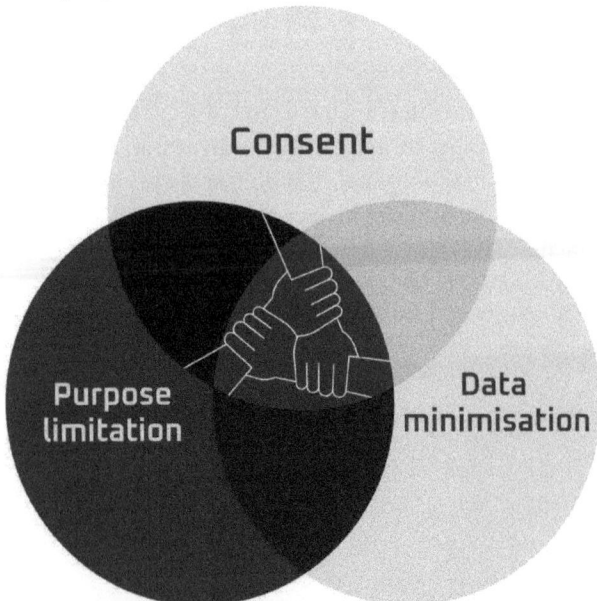

These two principles are interconnected. Together with the consent principle, they form a holy trinity of data protection: Only collect the data you actually need (data minimization), be clear about what you will use it for (purpose limitation), and ask permission first (consent).

And you know what is particularly beautiful about these principles? They are good for business too. First, it costs money to store data. Second, it is easier to stay organized when you are not hoarding a bunch of unnecessary information. Third—and perhaps most importantly—it builds trust. In an era when people are becoming increasingly aware of how their data gets misused, you stand out positively by showing that you respect their privacy.

Getting your house in order

But understanding the principles is not sufficient. You also need processes in place for how you handle personal data in practice. Picture a well-run shop on a quiet street. Outside, the digital blizzard howls, with data flying every which way between different services and platforms. But inside your shop, it is warm and cozy. The fire crackles in the tiled stove, and in the back office, you have everything perfectly organized—every paper and file in its place.

When a customer walks through the door wanting to know what information you have about them, you can easily pull out what they are looking for. Just as you keep track of your physical inventory, you have complete control over the data you manage, because that is exactly what you are doing—managing it. It is not your data; you are just borrowing it. And just as you keep your storefront tidy and inviting, you ensure your website is transparent about how you handle visitors' information.

As you will recall, the GDPR gives people the right to request information from you at any time about what personal data you have about them and how you use it, and if they wish, to ask you to delete it. You then have one month to respond.

Without clear processes and good organization, this quickly becomes a stress point.

But how do you know you have got your house in order? And how can you quickly prove it to, say, the IMY if they come knocking?

The answer is simple: You document your processes. It is like having an operating manual for how the shop should be run. Except in this case, it is a register of how you handle personal data. The register is your internal compass document. It should show how you think about the data you collect (data minimization), what you use it for (purpose limitation), and what lawful bases you rely on (like consent or contract). And if you share data with other companies or service providers (Google, Meta, HubSpot, etc.), that should be documented here too.

Note that the register is not the same thing as your privacy policy—the text you might have on your website that tells visitors how you handle personal data. Your privacy policy is your public promise to customers and leads. It can be creative and engaging, but it does not replace the need for an internal process document.

Let us return to our shop analogy: The privacy policy is like the storefront and the information you make visible to customers. It should be clear and inviting. Your register of processing activities is more like the operations manual of the shop—the one that describes everything from how to count the till to where the spare keys are kept. You need both external transparency and internal order.

Risk on the menu

Okay. Processes locked down? Check.
Understanding of core principles? Check.
What is next?
Now it is time to talk about risk.

Even when you do everything right, there is always risk involved when handling personal data. I am not talking about the risk of getting slapped with a hefty fine from the supervisory authority—though it is certainly a factor to consider. The real risk is about people's fundamental rights and freedoms.

Imagine you run an online pharmacy. Collecting information about which medications your customers buy is necessary to deliver the products. But if the information falls into the wrong hands, it can have serious consequences for the individual. That is what happened when two Swedish pharmacies ended up paying millions for sharing sensitive personal data with Facebook through its tracking pixel.[94]

In the GDPR, risk is about identifying and preventing potential threats to people's right to privacy. This could be anything from the risk of data breaches to the risk of information being shared without consent. Sometimes the risks are obvious—like with sensitive information about health or political opinions. Other times they can be more subtle, like when different data points combined can reveal information about a person they do not want to share.

In some cases, when the risk level is deemed high, the GDPR requires you to conduct a special impact assessment before you start collecting or processing personal data. That might sound cumbersome, but it is really just common sense systematized: What could go wrong? How serious would it be? And what can we do to prevent it?

Risk is therefore a central concept in data protection, not just in the GDPR but also in similar legislation like the CCPA in California. And it is actually a pretty practical framework to

---

[94] Apoteket AB: Received a penalty fee of 37 million kronor. Apohem AB: Received a penalty fee of 8 million kronor. Both companies used Meta's analytics tool, the Meta pixel, which led to more personal data than intended being transferred to Meta. The IMY determined that the companies had not taken appropriate technical and organizational measures to protect customers' personal data, resulting in these fines.

work from when you as a marketer want to adopt a more privacy-focused approach.

And speaking of risk. To make it easier to navigate data protection in a marketing context, I have developed a risk-based framework. By introducing three personas—*Hard Core Eleanor, Medium Megan, and Risky Ricky*—you get a framework to work from. This is not about judging which level is "best," but about understanding what choices you need to make depending on your business conditions and ambitions. Each of these personas represents different ways to balance marketing opportunities against the risks that come with handling personal data.

Hard Core Eleanor
– The minimalist path

Hard Core Eleanor represents the most spartan approach to privacy-first marketing. She is the character who might feel the most inspiring, but also the most challenging. Picture a successful blogger who generates substantial income, has a devoted following, and whose business model requires almost no personal data.

Eleanor has chosen a radical strategy: to minimize data collection to nearly zero. Her website uses strictly first-party data, meaning it is Eleanor's domain, and Eleanor who collects information from each user directly.

She does not ask her users for names or other details either—all they need to provide, if they want to subscribe to her posts, is an email address.

Her website and blog are also hosted on her own servers. To collect email addresses and send newsletters, she uses the security-focused service Proton.

She uses no third-party tools or tracking pixels. If she uses web analytics, she does so through a privacy-focused tool like Fathom, where the visitors behind the statistics are anonymized.

Her motto:
- Why complicate things?

Her measure of success:
- Bank statements.

When affiliate revenue rolls in each month, she knows her content works. She does not need complex analytics tools to confirm it. The UTM codes linked to affiliate links are her only concession. But only her affiliate partners see how they perform and pay her accordingly. Her readers can clearly see that the site contains such links, and that she can earn money if visitors choose to buy something through those links.

She also allows sponsored content with a native feel. And they are clearly marked.

Eleanor has built her brand over a long time, is known within her niche, and is also a popular speaker and podcast guest.

When Eleanor publishes a book, all data handling goes through the publisher. Collaboration requests are handled via email or phone.

Analogue Rogue

There are naturally degrees within the Hard Core Eleanor persona. In her most extreme form, she can be called an Analogue Rogue, where she continuously works to develop a kind of digital sovereignty with strong cybersecurity thinking.

Eleanor's approach to privacy is part of her business strategy and has helped strengthen her brand, because she has chosen to showcase it in various creative ways. For example, she has a page where she shows how visitors can easily verify that there are no scripts placing pixels on her domain.

Her followers know that when they visit her website, they will not be tracked or profiled. From the responses she gets, her visitors appreciate this. It strengthens her authenticity and trust, which is a currency worth more than "all the data in the world" for Analogue Rogue.

Advantages of Eleanor's Model

o   Minimal risk of data breaches or privacy violations.

o   No consent platform to manage.

o   No worries about compliance around data sharing.

o   A clear stance that builds credibility.

While Eleanor's approach dramatically reduces privacy and compliance risks, it is important to note that even minimal data collection—such as email addresses for newsletters or technical data like IP addresses in server logs—still falls under privacy regulations like the GDPR and ePrivacy. This means Eleanor must provide clear information about any data collected, ensure users can exercise their rights (such as unsubscribing or requesting data deletion), and maintain appropriate security measures.

Challenges

The challenges are apparent—Eleanor has essentially said no to classic digital data driven marketing with everything that it entails in terms of web analytics and optimization. To succeed with this approach, you have to "play the long game," as they say. And you need to think brand, brand, brand, and provide a sound offer.

Hard Core Eleanor is a name in her industry and niche; people want to be associated with her and spread her content. And she makes a good living from it.

Hard Core Eleanor thus embodies that less can be so much more. But she also represents an extreme on the privacy scale. For many businesses, her approach is neither practical nor desirable, which is why it is time to move on to Megan and subsequently Ricky.

Medium Megan – The balanced path

Medium Megan represents a middle ground of sorts. She runs a B-Corp-certified coffee roastery with both B2B and B2C sales, where ethical trade and sustainability are central. For Megan, the privacy issue is a natural part of the broader ethical compass of her company. She trades directly with small-scale coffee farmers and pays significantly above world market price to ensure quality and fair conditions.

"Protecting customers' privacy is as important as protecting farmers' rights," you would likely hear Megan say.

But Megan is also pragmatic with herself. She feels she needs to be where her customers are, even if it means compromises. Her approach to data protection and marketing can be described as "as much privacy as possible, as little tracking as necessary."

So what does Megan's toolkit look like?

For web analytics, she uses a privacy-secure platform like Piwik PRO, with built-in consent management. This gives her the insights she needs into her website without compromising visitors' privacy. For advertising, she relies primarily on contextual marketing through platforms like Kobler, where ads are shown based on context rather than tracking and profiling.

However—and here is where the pragmatism comes in—she also runs seasonal campaigns via Google Ads. It is a necessary evil in a market dominated by tech giants. However, she chooses to focus on iOS devices (Apple's ecosystem). This might seem contradictory since Apple has higher privacy standards, relatively speaking. Through their App Tracking Transparency (ATT) for mobile applications and their Intelligent Tracking Prevention for Safari, they have improved user privacy. This makes it harder for tracking-based programmatic advertising, since many users choose to deny tracking.

So why does Megan want to direct parts of her programmatic budget toward iOS users? Because Apple's approach has generated a cleaner advertising environment on iOS, and because their privacy solutions have led to reduced competition for users.

The industry is hyperactive on "the other side" where third-party cookies still work, as do the alternative ID solutions. So despite it being difficult to run retargeting and tracking-based targeting on iOS, it can be profitable, not least because iOS users have higher purchasing power. For Megan, it also feels a bit like choosing the lesser of two evils.

Email marketing is built entirely on first-party data through a reasonably GDPR-compliant platform like Acumbamail. Here she is extra careful—every email address in the system is based on consent through double opt-in, and people can always unsubscribe through a clear and simple link at the top of each newsletter.

Megan is also present on Instagram, but has chosen to stay off Meta's other big flagship, Facebook. On instagram she works solely with her personal account and takes a completely organic approach, i.e. no paid ads. Since she has been successful with her storytelling and network—she has won several barista competitions, for example, and has also managed to promote fantastic coffee bean production—her brand has a strong word-of-mouth. Additionally, her roastery is integrated with her café, which is mentioned among foodies worldwide.

Advantages of Megan's Approach

- o Strong credibility through consistent ethical behavior.
- o Ability to reach customers where they are without compromising on privacy too much.
- o Good regulatory compliance with reasonable effort.

While Megan's approach emphasizes privacy and ethical marketing, she still needs to ensure that all platforms and tools—especially those involving Google Ads and Instagram—are configured to respect user consent and comply with privacy regulations. Even with contextual and first-party data strategies, transparency about data collection, sharing, and user rights remains essential. Megan's regular collaboration with a Data Protection Officer helps her maintain this standard across both her B2B and B2C operations.

The Challenges

The challenges with Megan's higher risk tolerance are naturally that "reasonable effort" means more work for her than what it means for Hard Core Eleanor. Since she uses more services, like Google Ads, she needs to be more vigilant. She runs Piwik Pro with a built in CMP. To optimize her retargeting, she needs access to data on how the ads are preforming, which requires activating Google Consent Mode in the CMP. This integration works well with Piwik Pro and gives her significantly better control over her data than if she had chosen to use Google's entire ecosystem, including Google Analytics 4. Please note that she only uses Consent Mode in Basic Mode, not Advanced Mode. This means Google tags on her site respect user consent settings and do not send additional non-consented data to

Google for modeling or analytics purposes, further minimizing data sharing and enhancing user privacy.

By limiting her to only Google Ads and analyzing campaign performance through Piwik PRO, Megan reduces her exposure to Google's data-hungry ecosystem. While some data must still be shared with Google for ad delivery and basic conversion tracking, using Piwik PRO for analytics allows her to keep most user data within a more privacy-focused and controlled environment.

At the same time Megan needs to be a bit more vigilant, which is why she hires an independent Data Protection Officer, who helps her review her internal processes and external transparency at regular intervals. Megan views the DPO a bit like her accountant—but for data. She says it is a good investment, not least because she also uses this work in her sustainability reporting.

And speaking of "reasonable effort," let us check out our final persona—the most risk-tolerant character in the trio.

Risky Ricky – The ambitious path

If Eleanor represents minimalism and Megan the golden middle way, Risky Ricky is the one who has dared to dive headfirst into the data-driven marketing world—but with a twist. His e-commerce shoe business is doing well, to put it mildly, and he wants to use every modern marketing tool available. At the same time, he is determined to do it the right way.

"Privacy first doesn't mean privacy only," Ricky likes to say.

What makes Ricky "risky" is not that he is gambling or taking shortcuts. Quite the opposite. He has invested in both personnel and processes to handle complex digital marketing responsibly. But the more tools and data points you work with, the bigger the challenge becomes to keep everything under control.

Let us look at how Ricky has built his operation:

First and foremost, he has a full-time Data Protection Officer (DPO). This is not just a formal position—the DPO is deeply involved in all strategic decisions concerning data handling and marketing. At her side is a strategic media buyer, whose main job is ensuring that all paid advertising follows both legal requirements and the company's own ethical guidelines.

For web analytics, Ricky runs Google Analytics 4 with Consent Mode v2 in server-side mode. (At least so far. He has decided it may soon be time to replace Google Analytics with a solution like Piwik PRO, especially given the volatile global landscape and the growing importance of data ownership.) This is a technically advanced setup that requires significant resources to implement and maintain but provides better control over data flows. He has chosen an Enterprise-level CMP specifically adapted for e-commerce that can handle complex consent flows. While server-side tracking and Consent Mode v2 provide greater control and transparency, Ricky ensures that all data sent to external platforms is covered by user consent, and that no technical workarounds undermine the users' choices.

Ricky's marketing mix is extensive:

- o Paid advertising on Meta and Google.
- o Influencer partnerships with carefully selected partners.
- o Contextual marketing as a complement.
- o Email marketing based on first-party data.
- o Organic search engine optimization, which remains effective even as large language model-based search tools evolve.
- o Affiliate program with strict quality control.

For each channel, there are documented processes and controls. For example, all influencer partnerships must be approved by both the legal department and the DPO to ensure data sharing happens properly. Every new marketing tool or partner undergoes a comprehensive due diligence process before it can be implemented. All influencer and third-party partnerships are governed by formal data processing agreements and subject to regular privacy reviews, ensuring compliance with GDPR and other relevant regulations.

A particular focus lies on first-party data. Ricky has built a sophisticated loyalty program where customers get clear benefits in exchange for sharing more information about their preferences. All data collection happens with explicit consent, and customers can see and control what information the company has about them at any time through a special "privacy portal" on the website. Customers are regularly informed of their rights and can easily update or withdraw their consent at any time, in line with best practices under the GDPR.

Ricky's approach has its challenges:

- o Costs for personnel and systems.
- o Complex processes that can slow time-to-market.
- o Constant need for training and updates.
- o Risk of missing something in the extensive infrastructure.
- o Continuous need for documentation and follow-up.

To make all this work, Ricky has developed a systematic approach to data protection, which integrates privacy thinking into all parts of the business. It is not just about following rules but about building a culture where respect for customer privacy goes hand in hand with effective marketing.

A typical week for Ricky's team might include:

- o Review of consent statistics from the CMP.
- o Checking updated placement reports from ad networks.
- o Quality control of data flows in GA4.
- o Coordination with the DPO on new marketing initiatives.
- o Updating documentation and processes.
- o Training new hires on privacy routines.

But for Ricky, this is not just an operational machine—it is strategic business intelligence. As an entrepreneur and business leader, he sees it as crucial to understand where the market is heading. Reports from supervisory authorities and watch dog organizations therefore land directly on his and the board's desk.

"When Adalytics shows how unreliable data from the major platforms can be, then we as marketers must start questioning the premise of retargeting. Because this means we are wasting money."

That is why Ricky has chosen to keep all marketing in-house. His DPO and strategic media buyer function as a kind of early warning system. Their weekly review of placement reports and data flows do not only provide operational control, they also provide insights into how sustainable different marketing channels are in the long term.

"We live in a reality where a few tech giants dictate the terms for digital marketing," Ricky explains. "As an entrepreneur, I do not like monopolies—they stifle innovation and create vulnerabilities. When we follow the lawsuits against Google and see how Meta is losing trust capital, then we must also prepare for, and work toward, a web where more sound services can grow and improve the online marketplace, we are so dependent on."

This strategic perspective permeates the entire operation. When the board discusses long-term investments, privacy and data protection are always on the agenda—not as a cost or obstacle, but as part of the company's risk management and future-proofing.

"We're seeing how the market is changing," says Ricky. "Consumers are becoming more aware, regulations are tightening to some degree, and technical restrictions like Apple's ATT did shake up the entire industry. Those who will survive long-term must have a handle on all these aspects."

It is an extensive machine that requires continuous maintenance. But for Ricky, it is worth the effort. His conviction is that tomorrow's winners will be those who succeed in combining effective data-driven approaches with genuine respect for customers' privacy.

"We see privacy as a competitive advantage," he explains. "Our customers should know that even though we use advanced technology to give them a better experience, we always respect their choices and privacy."

Privacy first, second and last

The point of Eleanor, Megan, and Ricky is that this is an approach—a framework for finding a risk level that works for your business, your customers, and your goals. But above all, it is about seeing marketing for what it really is: a strategic function that drives the company's long-term development.

Privacy-first marketing gives you something, or encourages you to take something, that has become increasingly rare in our industry: time to think. Time to build systems that last. Time to make deliberate choices about which tools you use and why. This is not just philosophical—it is practical business strategy, like implementing proper accounting practices or conducting regular audits. Yes, it requires upfront investment and ongoing discipline. But just as you would not run a business without financial controls, you cannot build sustainable growth without data governance.

Consider this: performance marketers pour millions into Facebook ads while operating on platforms that Adalytics has shown produce unreliable data, where Meta allegedly makes calculated choices to undermine user privacy, and where Apple's ATT has already disrupted measurement overnight. That is not strategic—that is building a house on shifting sand. Privacy-first marketing is about constructing your foundation on something more solid.

For too long, marketers have been pressured to deliver quick results by exploiting all available data points, regardless of how they were collected or what risks this created for the business. But in a world where consumers are more aware and skeptical, where regulatory requirements are tightening, and where technical restrictions are reshaping the entire landscape, an eat-all-you-can approach is not just ethically unappetizing, it is a business liability.

The evidence is already there. Even Hard Core Eleanor is not some far-fetched archetype. The Polish blogger, Piotr Korzeniowski talked about, who generates millions annually after stripping his website completely bare proves otherwise. No tracking, no third-party tools, just content and bank statements. He is so transparent about his success that he publishes his tax returns on his blog.

Privacy-first marketing wants you to flip the perspective. Instead of seeing data protection as a limitation, see it as an opportunity to build stronger, more trustworthy relationships with the people that is your market. It means every data point you collect has a clear purpose, every tool you use is carefully selected, and every campaign respects your customers' privacy and choice.

As marketers, we are not just content pushers and number crushes supporting the sales team—we are the company's primary link to its customers and community. When we take a stand for sustainable business practices through a privacy-first approach, we signal that we value long-term relationships over short-term gains. We show that we are building something that can withstand regulatory changes, platform disruptions, and shifting consumer expectations.

However, prioritizing data protection is not about satisfying everyone or finding the perfect balance. At the end of the day, privacy and integrity is about honest assessment: What can you control? What are the real risks? And what kind of business do you want to build? But it is also about knowing that in a marketplace dominated by a few tech giants who dictate the terms for digital marketing, privacy-first marketing is about taking back some of that control. Thus, a privacy first approach is not only a vote for a more well-functioning web. But that in itself should be enough.

18. The trust factor

On January 23, 2025, a historic judgment was handed down in the British High Court. A former gambling addict had sued Sky Betting & Gaming for using his personal data for profiling and targeted marketing. The court ruled in his favor[95]. The judgment establishes that consent to data collection and marketing must be genuine and informed. The company in question had failed to achieve this. But the consent-part is only the top of this rather chilling iceberg, because who in their right mind would ever consent to a machine that assigned each user around 500 data points that were updated in real time? And who would then use them to build predictive models that could forecast which customers were most susceptible to what? Would you say yes to a system, which the more you gambled, the more data they collected and the better they got at using the information against you, triggering you to play even more?

So, Sky Betting & Gaming (SBG) was not just running a gambling site with some tracking pixels thrown in. They had built what the court documents reveal as a sophisticated hybrid operation—part gambling company, part adtech platform. And this hybrid model did not merely collect data to serve ads— indeed they collected gambling behavior data to engineer even more gambling behavior. In other words, when their systems detected that someone was gambling in the early morning hours (a recognized indicator of problem gambling), their marketing algorithms interpreted this as "a cue that that is a particularly productive time to send marketing to that individual." Yeah, let that sink in.

Oh, and since their own data sources were not enough, obviously, they combined their internal gambling data with third-party adtech services from companies like Google,

---

[95] RTM v Bonne Terre Limited,[2025] EWHC 93 (KB) (23 January 2025), available at: https://www.awo.agency/files/RTM-v-Bonne-Terre-judgment.pdf

Lotame, and Revenue Science to create what the court described as a "fast-moving marketing-saturated environment" designed to REALLY keep problem gamblers gambling. You simply cannot make this up.

Nevertheless, not all adtech is created equal, but the lack of transparency and the difficulty for lawmakers, marketers and any mere mortal seems to be what has sustained and allowed villains like SBG to think it is a good idea to do what they do, or for Meta to become too big and ruthless for any well-functioning democracy to handle. So, it all seems to boil down to the classic:

Why do they do it?
Because they can.

And even when they cannot (and get caught), they can afford the fines. So here we are. Sky Betting & Gaming could operate this way for years not because they were particularly clever, but because the entire adtech infrastructure is designed to be incomprehensible.

As Garcia explains, this opaqueness does not only enable predatory practices and violate the basic human right to privacy. In addition, it systematically diverts advertising dollars away from quality publishers into a labyrinth of middlemen and fraudulent sites.

But this book is evidently not called *What is Wrong with AdTech*. It is called "Privacy First Marketing," because I started this journey genuinely wanting to understand how we could get the whole privacy thing right as marketers, companies, and brands. And while we sure as hell can do a lot to save our own face, protect brand value, and help to mitigate embarrassing and dangerous data breaches, we also need to cut ourselves some slack and be realistic about our leverage.

No one can single-handedly fix a dysfunctional and often corrupt surveillance-based digital economy. But by seeing the bigger picture, we can begin to ask for the transparency that

Garcia advocates for regarding where we put our money. No, this book is not about adtech; it is all intertwined. We cannot make sense of anything if we do not zoom out once in a while and remind ourselves how the land lays and what the forest actually looks like.

And even if you do not care that much about privacy, you probably think monopolies are bad for, well, everybody, including the monopolies themselves. You probably also believe that a sound marketplace on the web, where everybody plays by the same rules with transparency and accountability, is a no-brainer. But today, we do not have that. Today, we as companies and brands can only run sustainable online businesses as far as the big players allow us to, on a marketplace rigged by their rules.

Legal scholar Lawrence Lessig identified decades ago that "code is law." The way platforms are designed, their architecture, algorithms, and technical choices, function as a form of regulation. Take for example, when Meta very recently was revealed to have programmed its apps (Instagram and Facebook) to open local network ports on Android phones, to track users even when they were browsing in incognito mode with VPNs enabled, or after clearing cookies.[96] By doing this, they did not just build a (non-compliant) product feature, you could argue they created their new rules about what privacy means on the web.

The localhost tracking issue is quite fascinating since Meta was shown to leverage technical loopholes that traditional privacy protection systems on Android phones are not designed to handle. Normally, your browser and your apps operate in

---

[96] Aniketh Girish (IMDEA Networks Institute & Universidad Carlos III de Madrid), Gunes Acar (Radboud University), Narseo Vallina-Rodriguez (IMDEA Networks Institute & Universidad Carlos III de Madrid), Nipuna Weerasekara (KU Leuven), Tim Vlummens (KU Leuven), "Covert Web-to-App Tracking via Localhost on Android" (June 2025), available at: https://localmess.github.io

isolation, with limited ways to share data directly. But Meta's method breaks this separation by having their Pixel script on websites (which is embedded on over 22 percent of the world's most visited sites) communicate through the phone's local network interface directly with Meta's apps running in the background. So basically, every time you visit a website with the Meta Pixel embedded, Meta is able to track your activities and connect them to your Facebook or Instagram account. Even if you clear cookies, use incognito mode, or turn on a VPN, your activity on these websites is still secretly linked to your identity.

Is there a sliver of a silver lining? Well, this only works if you have the actual Meta apps installed and if you are on an Android phone. Clearly, this level of technical sophistication and invasive data collection does not happen by accident. It requires coordinated engineering efforts, strategic product decisions, and executive approval—showing that privacy erosion is embedded by design, not a side effect.

Recent whistleblower testimony from Sarah Wynn-Williams, Meta's former director of global public policy, helped dispel any remaining illusion that such problematic systems arise by accident. Her Senate testimony revealed that Meta executives, allegedly, deliberately built and adapted their products to comply with the Chinese government's strict censorship and regulatory demands, creating a version that was "safe" for China but compromised on privacy and national security in ways not seen in Western markets. This was not "move fast and break things"—this was a calculated strategy reflecting a corporate culture willing to make ethically fraught decisions to gain market access.[97]

---

[97] Sarah Wynn-Williams, Testimony before the Senate Judiciary Subcommittee on Crime and Counterterrorism (9 April 2025), as reported in "Meta whistleblower tells senators Facebook worked 'hand in glove' with Chinese government to censor posts" CBS News (10 April 2025), available at: https://www.cbsnews.com/news/meta-whistleblower-testimony-senate-judiciary-subcommittee/; see also "Meta silenced a whistleblower. Now she's talking to Congress." The Washington Post (10 April 2025), available at:

Adtech players like Meta and Google have been able to grow in a regulatory vacuum, which would have been unthinkable in any other sector. Imagine if airline manufacturers could design planes without safety oversight, or pharmaceutical companies could distribute drugs without clinical trials. The idea is absurd. Nevertheless, that is essentially what Section 230, and the absence of privacy guardrails created for the tech industry in the United States[98]. And since the web knows no borders, the effects of this have been global, despite the EU having become a pebble in their shoe.

Meta currently holds the record for GDPR fines in the EU— over €2 billion in penalties for privacy violations (as of 2025). But here is the kicker: It is hard not to state that their business model requires them to violate privacy laws to function effectively. The more personal data they collect, the better their targeting becomes, the more they can charge advertisers. And their AI development and Metaverse vision only amplify the need for more invasive data collection. It creates a perverse incentive where platform owners like Meta have chosen to frame privacy protection as a threat to free speech and innovation[99]. However, the issue is not whether people should be able to share information online. It is whether tech giants should be able to harvest the information without meaningful consent to manipulate what users see and think.

---

https://www.washingtonpost.com/technology/2025/04/09/meta-wynn-williams-facebook-china-congress/

[98] Section 230 shields platforms from lawsuits over user content, and—with no strong federal privacy laws and only until recently at the state level—tech companies have been able to collect and use personal data with almost no oversight.

[99] See Simon Milner (Facebook UK Public Policy Director), quoted in "Facebook: 'Data laws could stifle innovation'" Marketing Week (17 October 2012), available at: https://www.marketingweek.com/facebook-data-laws-could-stifle-innovation/; Mark Zuckerberg and Daniel Ek, "CEOs of Meta and Spotify Say EU Regulations 'Stifle Innovation'" PYMNTS (23 August 2024), available at: https://www.pymnts.com/artificial-intelligence-2/2024/ceos-of-meta-and-spotify-say-eu-regulations-stifle-innovation/

We are living in a landscape where algorithmic systems, fueled by unprecedented personal data collection, shape not only what we buy but also what we believe and how we vote.

This is not sustainable. No democracy can function when a handful of unaccountable tech giants control both the platforms where citizens get their information and the algorithms that determine what information they see. Or that smaller players run the same race. The SBG case reveals what happens when digital surveillance meets human vulnerability. The Meta revelations show what happens when it meets geopolitical power.

Either we admit that code is law and accept that platform programmers are our unelected lawmakers, or we reclaim that authority through transparency requirements, interoperability standards, and genuine privacy protections. As marketers, we are not passive observers in this process. Every budget decision we make, every platform we choose, every data practice we accept is a vote for what kind of (digital) future we want.

About the Author

When I started writing this book about two years ago, it was mostly to satisfy my own curiosity. To explain things to myself, really. I figured it might turn into maybe 50-100 pages at most—a small handbook about cookies or the like.

But the deeper I dug ... Well, you know how it goes. It was a rabbit hole. And now here I am, hoping that if you have made it this far, it has made you wiser. Maybe you have some thoughts or questions? I would love to hear from you—I want to know what you think. Did I miss something important?

My best friend, Emmett Norling, keeps telling me I need to write something about myself, so readers know who is behind the book. But honestly, I am not sure it is necessary. If you have read this far, you probably have a pretty good sense of who the author is.

Though I suppose I should mention that this journey into the infinite world of data protection has led me to co-found a software company called Peak Privacy. There, my brilliant colleague András Marczell and I offer an agent that automatically tests mobile applications for companies as if it were a human user. Because if you think website tracking seems tangled, it is nothing compared to how mobile apps work. Unfortunately.

Problems and challenges exist to be solved, however. And I think it is what we all need to remind ourselves when the world feels overwhelming. You do not eat an elephant in one bite—you take it piece by piece. One person cannot fix everything, but everyone can do their bit.

If we just keep that in mind, there are no limits to how we, together and individually, can push back against the Matrix and save democracy.

Vibeke Specht
Hvalsø, Denmark, August 2025
vibeke@peakprivacy.eu

www.ingramcontent.com/pod-product-compliance
Ingram Content Group UK Ltd.
Pitfield, Milton Keynes, MK11 3LW, UK
UKHW011846181125
9046UKWH00022B/230

9 788797 643808